Puppet Pizzazz!

Using Puppets to Spark Interest and Learning in the Early-Childhood Classroom

Written by
Rita Jamieson

Editor: Kim Cernek
Illustrator: Catherine Yuh
Cover Photographer: Michael Jarrett
Designer: Terri Lamadrid
Cover Designer: Moonhee Pak
Art Director: Tom Cochrane
Project Director: Carolea Williams

Special Thanks to:
Delores Burris,
University of California, Riverside,
for her encouragement

● ●

CTP © 2000 Creative Teaching Press, Inc., Huntington Beach, CA 92649
Reproduction of activities in any manner for use in the classroom and not for commercial sale is permissible.
Reproduction of these materials for an entire school or for a school system is strictly prohibited.

Table of Contents

Introduction 4

Language and Literacy

Story Time
    Owl Feather-Duster Puppet 6
    Snake Sock Puppet 8
    Brown Bear Mask 10
    Fuzzy Monster Golf-Sock Puppet 12
    Ladybug Paper-Plate Puppet 14

Poetry Pals
    Bunny Glove Puppet 16
    Elephant Sleeve Puppet 18
    Chatterbox, the Box Puppet 20
    Bird Finger Puppets 22
    Fuzzy Caterpillar Stick Puppet 24

Listening and Speaking Skills
    Turtle Sock Puppet 26
    Spider Glove Puppet 28
    Owl Mitten Puppet 30
    Splatter-Shield Mask 32
    Wiggle Worm Puppet 34

Skills Development

Shapes
    Pee-Wee, the Ping-Pong Paddle Puppet 36
    Sergeant Shape Puppet 38
    Clown Bottle Puppet 40

Colors
    Fish Stick Puppet 42
    Turkey Glove Puppet 44
    Perry Parrot Sock Puppet 46

Alike and Different
    Flip and Flop Kitchen Sponge Puppets 48
    Wooden Spoon and Fork Puppets 50
    Flower Finger Puppets 52

Numbers
    Elephant Sock Puppet 54
    Peter Pointer Sleeve Puppet 56
    Bunny Finger Puppets 58

Music and Motion

Songs
- Presto, the Pop-up Puppet 60
- Garden Man Coat-Hanger Puppet 62
- Duck Car-Wash-Mitt Puppet 64
- Dog Stuffed-Animal Puppet 66

Movement
- Dinosaur Glove Puppet 68
- Animal Paper-Sack Puppets 70
- Tiger Kitchen-Mitt Puppet 72
- Wild Thing Grocery-Sack Mask 74

Games
- Simon, the Sponge-Paintbrush Puppet 76
- Snail Stocking Puppet 78
- Stoplight Sponge Puppet 80
- Ace, the Racquet Puppet 82

Self-Esteem

Exploring Emotions
- Silhouette Felt Puppet 84
- Peek-a-Boo Stick Puppet 86
- Anyone Felt Puppet 88

Praise
- High-Five Flyswatter Puppet 90
- Butterfly Finger Puppet 92
- Drizzle, the Watering-Can Puppet 94

Problem Solving
- Mop-Head Puppet 96
- Fuzzy Wuzzy Cuddlebug Slipper Puppet 98
- Happy/Sad Sylvester Stick Puppet 100

Classroom Management

Transition Tools
- Mr. Peekers Stick Puppet 102
- Paddy, the Paddleball Puppet 104
- Wibble Wobble Bathroom-Brush Puppet 106
- Mr. Redhead Yarn Puppet 108

Rest Time
- Rooster Stick Puppet 110
- Miss Whisper Sleeve Puppet 112
- Rock-a-Bye Baby Puppet 114
- Buster Brush Puppet 116

Cleanup
- Mr. Crackers Paintbrush Puppet 118
- Pig Sponge Puppet 120
- Dilly, the Duster Puppet 122
- Bumblebee Paper-Plate Puppet 124

Reproducible Patterns 126

Introduction

Can you get your hands *on* a garden glove, a paper bag, and a sock? Now, get your hands *into* these everyday items, dress them up with some simple craft supplies, and you are ready to spark interest and learning in your early-childhood classroom!

Puppet Pizzazz! is your guide to creating unique, whimsical puppets in an instant. Use these puppets to present curriculum and manage your class in fun and exciting ways. The children in your class will be delighted as they interact with these playful characters that you create and bring to life.

Why Puppets?

Integrate puppets into your daily program to address your early-childhood learners' various developmental needs, including the following:

- **Multiple Modalities**
  The use of puppets stimulates children's auditory, visual, and kinesthetic learning modalities, enabling you to introduce information, skills, and concepts and promote optimal learning retention. When children interact with puppets, they are encouraged to think creatively and use their imagination.

- **Nonthreatening Atmosphere**
  Puppets create a nonthreatening environment for children to investigate new ways of doing things, to explore unfamiliar situations, and to problem-solve.

- **Self-Esteem Building**
  Puppets also empower children to express their feelings. Children tend to lose their inhibitions when they know that a puppet, and not themselves, is the focus of attention. Children then feel free to explore a range of emotions, which contributes to improved self-esteem.

- **Verbal Exploration**
  Puppets also encourage verbal exploration. Children can practice and develop their speaking and listening skills as they use puppets to retell a story, recite poetry, sing a song, respond to literature, rhyme, and manipulate sounds. Children will also develop language skills when they use puppets to count; observe scientific experiments; and identify shapes, colors, and numbers.

- **Terrific Management Tools**
  Puppets can become terrific tools for classroom management. Use a puppet to give a direction, lead a game, make an announcement, begin rest time, initiate a cleanup session, or make any other transition during your day.

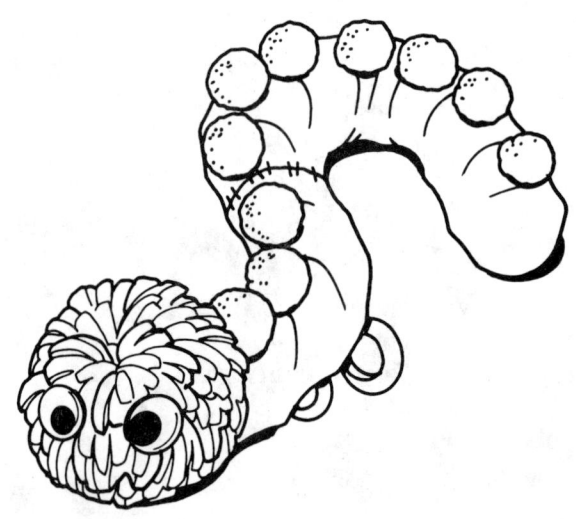

Making Puppets

Use the simple, clear, and easy-to-follow directions in *Puppet Pizzazz!* to create 60 puppets. Each puppet is made with common household items and art supplies. As an added bonus, ideas for making clever variations of each puppet are also included. Use your own imagination and creativity to transform the puppets in this book into those that will best meet the needs of your early-childhood classroom.

Begin by obtaining a glue gun and collecting puppet-making materials, including ricrac, buttons, wiggly eyes, pom-pom balls, lace, fabric, fur, pipe cleaners, sequins, and craft foam. Look in familiar places for supplies to add to your collection. For example, ask a paint store to donate paint-stirring sticks, or search garage sales for "treasures" such as slippers, stuffed animals, and other simple items that you can transform into a puppet.

Lesson Features

Reading recommendations and suggested songs are also provided for each puppet. Each title reflects the interests and developmental needs of children in an early-childhood classroom. Some of these recommended titles are used as part of activities in this book, while others are listed as supplemental resources.

Be creative, use your imagination, and have fun!

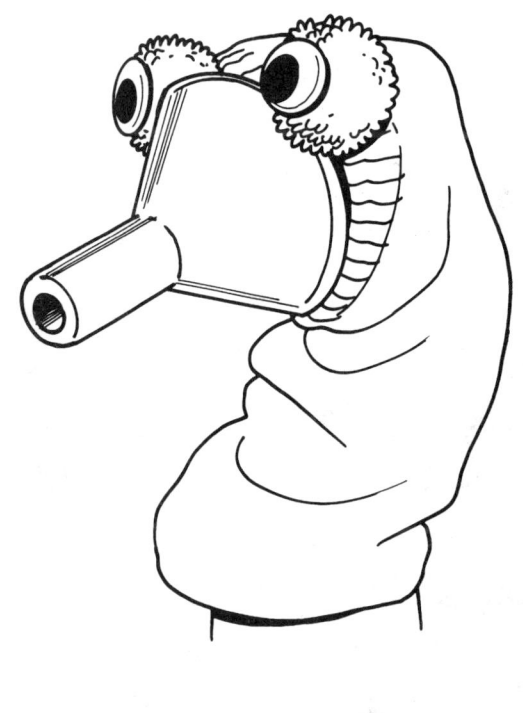

Owl Feather-Duster Puppet

Materials
circular object (e.g., lid of small container)
brown and yellow felt
scissors
glue gun
feather duster
wiggly eyes

Directions
Trace around a circular object on a piece of brown felt. Cut out the circle, and glue it to the front of a feather duster. Glue on a pair of wiggly eyes. Cut a beak from a piece of yellow felt, and glue it onto the circle below the eyes.

Variation
Place the circle with the beak and eyes at the top of the feather duster to create an ostrich puppet.

Reading Recommendations
Goodnight Owl by Pat Hutchins
Lazy Ozzie by Michael Coleman
The Owl and the Pussycat by Jan Brett
Owl at Home by Arnold Lobel
Owl at Night by Ann Whitford Paul
Owl Babies by Martin Waddell

Song Suggestions
"Two Little Owls" from *Little White Duck* by Burl Ives (Columbia Records)

Try This Puppet on for Size

Materials
Lazy Ozzie by Michael Coleman
different-sized objects

Read aloud *Lazy Ozzie*. In the story, Ozzie is too lazy to fly to the ground, so he jumps from one animal to a shorter animal until he reaches it. Use this story to discuss size relationships with children. Present two objects of a different size (e.g., a book and a pencil). Have the Owl Feather-Duster Puppet say *Whoo knows which is bigger, the book or the pencil?* Invite a volunteer to use the puppet to point to the larger object. Show children two new objects, and repeat the activity. Or, try using children instead of objects. For example, call two children to stand before the class, and say *Whoo knows who is taller, Caleb or Martin?*

Oldies but Goodies

Materials
storybooks

Use the Owl Feather-Duster Puppet to introduce a book that the class enjoyed in the past but has not heard in a while. Hold up the book, use the puppet to "dust off" the book, and say *Here's a story that has been collecting dust on the shelf because we haven't read it in so long! Let's dust it off and hear what we've been missing.* Encourage children to use the puppet during free-choice time. This will inspire them to revisit some of their own favorite stories.

Snake Sock Puppet

Materials

Mouth pattern (page 126)
scissors
men's brightly colored athletic or soccer sock
cardboard
felt
glue
wiggly eyes

Directions

Cut off the toe of the sock. Make a copy of the Mouth pattern, and cut it out. Trace the pattern onto cardboard and onto a piece of felt, and cut out the pieces. Glue the felt piece to one side of the cardboard, and fold the cardboard in half. Place glue along the edges of the cardboard on the side covered with felt. Press the edges of the cut end of the sock along the glue on the felt to form a mouth. Glue on wiggly eyes.

•••

Variation

Add construction paper legs and a forked tongue to create a lizard puppet.

Reading Recommendations

Jimmy's Boa Bounces Back by Trinka Hakes Noble
Snake Alley Band by Elizabeth Nygaard
Verdi by Janell Cannon
Will You Be My Friend? by Eric Carle

Song Suggestions

"Animal Quiz Part One" from *Can a Cherry Pie Wave Goodbye?* by Hap Palmer (Hap Palmer Recordings)
"Sally and the Swinging Snake" from *Sally and the Swinging Snake* by Hap Palmer (Educational Activities, Inc.)

Will You Be My Friend?

Materials

Will You Be My Friend? by Eric Carle

Use the Snake Sock Puppet to share the picture book *Will You Be My Friend?* Use the puppet to ask children which animal's tail appears on each page. Encourage children to tell which animals they would like to have for a friend.

Snake S-S-S-S Stories

Materials

sentence strips
pocket chart
chart paper
colored markers

Invite children to brainstorm a list of words that begin with *s*. Write each word on a sentence strip, and place the strips in a pocket chart. Ask children to use the words to create a class story, and write it on chart paper. Use a different colored marker to write words that begin with *s*. Explain to children that when they include several words that begin with the same sound in a sentence they are using alliteration. Have the Snake Sock Puppet "read" the story back to the class.

Brown Bear Mask

Materials

Bear pattern (page 127)
scissors
cardboard
black felt
glue
marker
tape
paint-stirring stick

Directions

Make a copy of the Bear pattern, and cut it out. Trace the pattern onto cardboard, and cut it out. Cut small holes for eyes. Cut out a nose and a mouth from black felt, and glue them to the cardboard to create a face. Use a marker to draw whiskers beside the nose. Tape a paint-stirring stick to the back for use as a handle.

• •

Variation

Trace the Bear pattern onto gray construction paper to create a koala bear puppet or onto white construction paper to create a polar bear puppet.

Reading Recommendations

Bears in the Night by Stan and Jan Berenstain
Brown Bear, Brown Bear, What Do You See? by Bill Martin Jr. and Eric Carle
A Bug, a Bear, and a Boy Go to School by David McPhail
Jesse Bear, What Will You Wear? by Nancy White Carlstrom

Song Suggestions

"The Bear and the Mountain" from *Shake a Leg* by Norman Foote (Youngheart Music)
"Brown Bear, Brown Bear, What Do You See?" from *Playing Favorites* by Greg & Steve (Youngheart Music)
"Teddy Bear" from *Make Believe* by Linda Arnold (Youngheart Music)

Have You Found the Sound?

Materials
Brown Bear, Brown Bear, What Do You See? by Bill Martin Jr. and Eric Carle

Use the Brown Bear Mask to give children some practice with phonemic awareness. Read aloud *Brown Bear, Brown Bear, What Do You See?* Hold up the mask, and say

> Brown bear, brown bear,
> What do you see?
> **It starts with /d/.**
> What can it be?

Encourage children to name the animal from the story that begins with /d/ (i.e., dog). Repeat the activity with another beginning sound, or change the boldfaced words in the verse to have children practice ending sounds (e.g., *It ends with /p/—* for sheep) or rhyming words (e.g., *It rhymes with hat—* for cat).

Brown Bear, Brown Bear, Whom Do You See?

Materials
Brown Bear, Brown Bear, What Do You See? by Bill Martin Jr. and Eric Carle

Arrange children in a circle. Read aloud *Brown Bear, Brown Bear, What Do You See?* Hold the Brown Bear Mask in front of your face, and say *Brown Bear, Brown Bear, whom do you see?* Look at the child sitting to your left, and say *I see (child's name) looking at me!* Hand the mask to the child you just named, and encourage him or her to repeat the chant with the name of the child to his or her left. Continue until each child has participated.

Story Time

Fuzzy Monster Golf-Sock Puppet

Materials
scissors
craft foam
glue gun
Velcro
plain golf sock

Directions
Cut out eyes, ears, a nose, a mouth, teeth, and hair from craft foam, and glue Velcro to each piece. Glue Velcro to the sock in the places where the eyes, ears, nose, mouth, teeth, and hair will go. Attach the facial features to the golf sock to create a face.

Variation
Attach wiggly eyes and a nose, a mouth, small pointed ears, and large pointed teeth cut from felt to a gray golf sock to create a wolf puppet.

Reading Recommendations
Five Little Monsters Went to School by Rozanne Lanczak Williams (Creative Teaching Press)
Go Away, Big Green Monster! by Ed Emberley
Huggly and the Toy Monster by Tedd Arnold
The Monster at the End of This Book by Jon Stone

Song Suggestions
"Monster Day" from *Peppermint Wings* by Linda Arnold (Youngheart Music)

Making Sense to a Monster

Materials

none

Use the Fuzzy Monster Golf-Sock Puppet to highlight four of the five senses (sight, hearing, taste, smell). Remove all facial features from the puppet. Say *What does Fuzzy Monster need to see?* Invite a child to place the eyes on the puppet. Revise the question to reflect other senses.

Go Away, Fuzzy Monster!

Materials

Go Away, Big Green Monster! by Ed Emberley

Read aloud *Go Away, Big Green Monster!* Retell the story, and invite children to join you. Remove each part of the Fuzzy Monster Golf-Sock Puppet when "directed" to do so by the children. For example, prompt children to say *Go away, scraggly hair!* and remove the hair from the puppet. Continue the activity until only the sock remains. Make the puppet and the book available for children to use in a free-choice period.

Story Time

Ladybug Paper-Plate Puppet

Materials
scissors
red and black felt
paper plate
paint-stirring stick
glue
pipe cleaner
buttons

Directions
Cut a piece of red felt to cover a paper plate, and cut a piece of black felt to cover a paint-stirring stick. Glue felt in place. Fold the plate in half (felt side out), insert the paint-stirring stick, and glue the edges of the plate together. Cut out dots from black felt, scatter them onto the red felt, and glue them in place. Cut a circle from black felt, and glue it to one end of the paint-stirring stick. Glue on pipe-cleaner antennae and button eyes.

Variation
Cover the plate with green felt and add other features (e.g., legs and wings) cut from construction paper to create a grasshopper puppet.

Reading Recommendations
Bugs by David A. Carter
The Bugs Go Marching by Rozanne Lanczak Williams (Creative Teaching Press)
The Grouchy Ladybug by Eric Carle

Song Suggestions
"Bugs Go Marching" from *Counting Kittens* by John Archambault and David Plummer (Creative Teaching Press)

Being Polite Is All Right!

Materials

The Grouchy Ladybug by Eric Carle

Read aloud *The Grouchy Ladybug*. Invite the class to help the Ladybug Paper-Plate Puppet retell the story. Assign individual children or small groups the parts of the yellow jacket, praying mantis, and other creatures from the story that meet the Grouchy Ladybug. Use the puppet to ask each child or small group *Want to fight?* Encourage children to paraphrase the response of the creature they are role-playing. Continue the activity until the puppet is "convinced" that it is much nicer (and wiser) to be friendly than grouchy!

The Friendly Ladybug

Materials

none

Use the Ladybug Paper-Plate Puppet to help put "grouchy" children into a good mood. Encourage a child who is having a bad day to tell the puppet about his or her problem. A few words of kindness, wisdom, and humor from the puppet will undoubtedly turn any child's frown into a smile!

Story Time

Bunny Glove Puppet

Materials

white cotton garden glove
scissors
needle
white and black thread
glue gun
wiggly eyes
pink and orange felt
pom-pom ball
marker

Directions

Cut off the pointer and pinky fingers from the glove. Fold down the thumb of the glove to form one of the bunny's "hands," and use a needle and white thread to stitch it in place. Stitch the pinky finger to the side opposite the thumb to create the other hand. The remaining two fingers are the ears. Glue below the ears wiggly eyes, ears cut from pink felt, a pom-pom ball for a nose, and black thread for whiskers. Use a marker to draw a mouth. Cut a carrot from a piece of orange felt, and glue it onto one of the hands. To manipulate the puppet, place your pointer and middle fingers into the ears.

Variation

Cut off the middle and ring fingers of a brown glove. Fold down the thumb to form a "hand," and use a needle and thread to stitch it in place. Stitch the pinky finger to the side opposite the thumb to create the other hand. Add features cut from brown felt to create a dog or cat puppet.

Reading Recommendations

Guess How Much I Love You by Sam McBratney
I Am a Little Rabbit by François Crozat
Little Rabbit's Loose Tooth by Lucy Bate
What Have You Done, Davy? by Brigitte Weninger

Song Suggestions

"Mr. Rabbit" from *Little White Duck* by Burl Ives (Columbia Records)
"Peter Cottontail" from *Holidays and Special Times* by Greg & Steve (Youngheart Music)

The Funny Bunny

Materials
none

Use the Bunny Glove Puppet to recite the following poem:
> The silly bunny with ears so funny
> Found a hole big and round.
> When a dog comes near,
> He perks up each ear
> And hops down under the ground.

Repeat the verse, and invite children to pantomime the actions of this "funny bunny." Invite children to create a new verse and act it out with the puppet.

A "Sense"itive Bunny

Materials
none

Use the Bunny Glove Puppet to lead a discussion about the five senses. Recite the poem below, and point to the part of the rabbit's body that relates to each sense word named. Ask children to point to the same parts of their own bodies.
> As I hopped back home one fine spring day,
> I discovered many things along the way.
> I **saw** one blue egg in a robin's nest.
> I **heard** two noisy ducklings who just wouldn't rest.
> I **touched** three woolly lambs as black as night.
> I **smelled** four pink roses opening to the light.
> I **tasted** five crunchy carrots growing in some dirt.
> The wonders of spring do keep my senses awake and alert!

Elephant Sleeve Puppet

Materials
scissors
gray sweatshirt
gray felt
glue gun
wiggly eyes

Directions
Cut off one sleeve of the sweatshirt at the shoulder, and fold the sleeve in half. The cuffed end will be the tip of the elephant's trunk. Cut out ears from gray felt, and glue them on either side of the sleeve below the fold. Glue wiggly eyes between the ears. Place your arm inside the cut end, and grasp the material within the sleeve to control the puppet.

Variation
Use a brown sweatshirt and felt and add white tusks cut from construction paper to create a woolly mammoth puppet.

Reading Recommendations
Five Minutes Peace by Jill Murray
Horton Hears a Who by Dr. Seuss
Little Elephant by Tana Hoban

Song Suggestions
"We Are Elephants" from *You Are Special* by Mister Rogers (Youngheart Music)
"When I See an Elephant Fly" from *Circus Magic* by Linda Arnold (Youngheart Music)
"Willoughby Wallaby Woo" from *More Singable Songs* by Raffi (Rounder Records)

Do the Elephant Stomp

Materials

blue tablecloth or piece of blue fabric (optional)

In advance, make five Elephant Sleeve Puppets. Ask five children to stand before the class. Give each of these children a puppet. Invite the class to join you as you chant the following verse, and encourage the first child to pantomime the actions:

__One elephant__ at the river
Going for a swim.
Clap, clap, stomp, stomp!
__She__ dove right in!

Change the boldfaced words to indicate that another elephant has joined the first. Chant the new verse, and ask the second child to join the first in pantomiming the actions. For example:

__Two elephants__ at the river
Going for a swim.
Clap, clap, stomp, stomp!
__They__ dove right in!

Continue changing the boldfaced words until all five children have participated. Invite five other children to stand before the class with a puppet, and repeat the activity. To give the "elephants" an authentic place to "swim" and "stomp," place a blue tablecloth or a piece of blue fabric on the floor to represent the river.

Poetry Pals

Chatterbox, the Box Puppet

Materials

small shirt box
scissors
glue gun
yarn
wiggly eyes
marker

Directions

Place the bottom half of a small shirt box upside down on a flat surface. Draw two lines widthwise across the middle of the box. The space between the two lines should equal the width of the sides of the box. Extend the lines down both sides of the box. Cut only the small lines on each side of the box. Cut out the piece on each side that is indicated in the diagram. Bend the box along the lines on the back so that a hollow space is created inside. This will be the mouth of the puppet. Glue on yarn for hair and wiggly eyes. Use a marker to draw a mouth.

Variation

Paint the box green and add pointed teeth cut from white construction paper to create a crocodile puppet.

Reading Recommendations

Anna Banana: 101 Jump Rope Rhymes by Joanna Cole
Let's Play: Traditional Games of Childhood by Camilla Gryski
Miss Mary Mack by Nadine Bernard Westcott
Mr. Chatterbox by Roger Hargreaves

Song Suggestions

"Jump Rope Song" from *ABC Chicka Boom with Me* by John Archambault and David Plummer (Creative Teaching Press)
"Miss May-ree Mack" from *Multicultural Children's Songs* by Ella Jenkins (Folkways/Smithsonian)

What's the Chatter?

Materials
>marker
>chart paper

Hide Chatterbox behind your back. Recite the following poem, and show the children the puppet when you say the last line:
>*She's a chatterbox.*
>*And she talks all day.*
>*But when she's shy she hides away.*
>*She hides her face. She hides her eyes.*
>*Then out she jumps and shouts SURPRISE!*

Have the puppet ask the class *What makes you feel shy?* Ask children why they think the puppet is named Chatterbox. Prompt children to identify times when it is appropriate for them to talk in class. Write children's ideas on chart paper, and refer to the chart when the class is being too noisy.

Keeping Time for a Hand-Clapping Rhyme

Materials
>none

Use Chatterbox to accompany familiar hand-clapping games, such as "Say, Say, Oh Playmate" or "Miss Mary Mack." Open and close the puppet's mouth to provide a beat for the songs. Encourage children to make up their own songs and clapping rhymes to perform for the rest of the class.

Poetry Pals

Bird Finger Puppets

Materials
scissors
men's black garden glove
yellow felt
glue gun
wiggly eyes

Directions
Cut off two fingers from the glove. Cut out two beaks from yellow felt, and glue one beak to each cutoff glove finger. Glue on wiggly eyes.

Variation
Add small whiskers cut from black thread and two small ears cut from gray felt to a gray glove to create mice finger puppets.

Reading Recommendations
Are You My Mother? by P. D. Eastman
Black Crow, Black Crow by Ginger Foglesong Guy
Clap Your Wings by P. D. Eastman
Feathers for Lunch by Lois Ehlert
Hand Rhymes by Marc Brown
Read Aloud Rhymes for the Very Young selected by Jack Prelutsky

Song Suggestions
"Bluebird" and "Two Little Blackbirds" from *Mainly Mother Goose* by Sharon, Lois, and Bram (Drive)
"Do the Bird" from *Dream Catcher* by Jack Grunsky (Youngheart Music)

The Mocking Birds

Materials

none

Use the Bird Finger Puppets to teach children this version of "Are You Sleeping?" Move each puppet to indicate which one is singing.

First Bird Puppet
Are you singing?
Little bird.
Your song is really cheerful.
Fly away.

Second Bird Puppet
Are you singing?
Little bird.
Your song is really cheerful.
Fly away.

Encourage children to sing the song and use their fingers to imitate the actions of the puppets. To extend learning, use the puppets to help children learn new words. Have one puppet introduce new vocabulary words (e.g., *butterfly, chrysalis, metamorphosis*), and have the second puppet lead the class in repeating the words.

Fly Away

Materials

none

Place a Bird Finger Puppet on the pointer finger of each of your hands. Recite the following rhyme and perform the actions:

Two little blackbirds	Place both puppets behind your back.
Sitting on a hill.	
One named Jack.	Place one puppet in front of you.
And one named Jill.	Place the other puppet in front of you.
Fly away Jack.	Place one puppet behind you.
Fly away Jill.	Place the other puppet behind you.
Come back Jack!	Place one puppet in front of you.
Come back Jill!	Place the other puppet in front of you.

Repeat the activity, and invite children to use their fingers to imitate the actions of the puppets as they sing along.

Fuzzy Caterpillar Stick Puppet

Materials

glue gun
pom-pom balls
2 small dowels or chopsticks
1" (2.5 cm) strips of felt
wiggly eyes
pipe cleaners

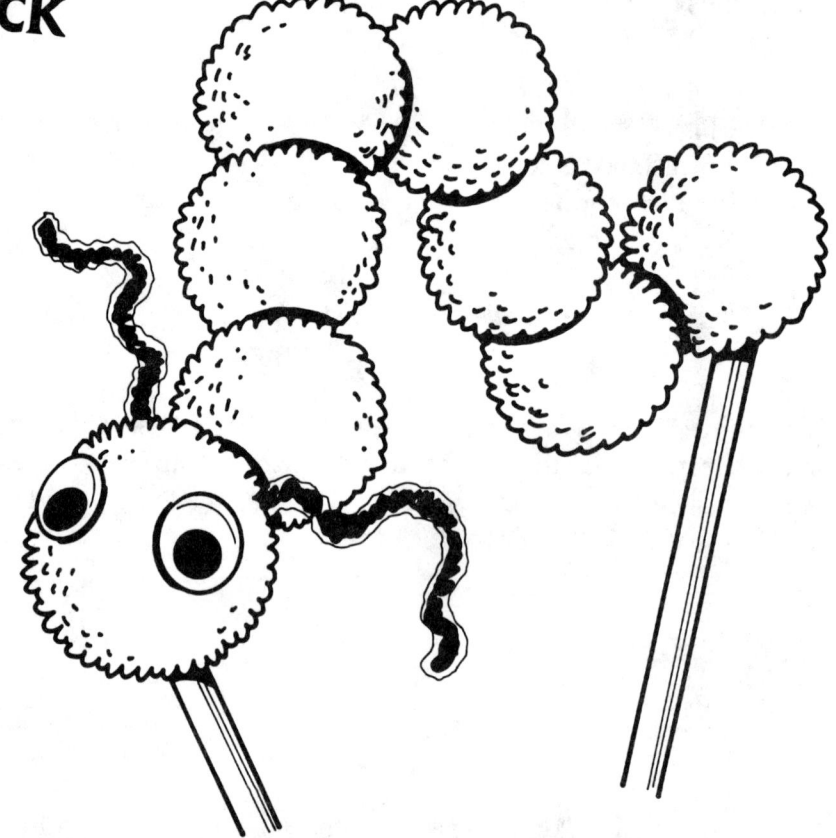

Directions

Glue together any number of pom-pom balls to form a "chain." Glue a dowel or chopstick to both the first and last pom-pom ball. Glue a thin strip of felt to the bottom of the dowels to protect children from harming themselves with the pointed edge. Glue wiggly eyes and pipe-cleaner antennae to the pom-pom ball at one end. To move the puppet, hold a dowel or chopstick in each hand, and turn the sticks with your fingertips.

•••

Variation

Instead of using pom-pom balls, attach a dowel or chopstick to each end of a small feather boa to create a snake puppet.

Reading Recommendations

The Caterpillar and the Polliwog by Jack Kent
Charlie the Caterpillar by Dom Deluise
I Am a Little Caterpillar by François Crozat
The Very Hungry Caterpillar by Eric Carle

Song Suggestions

"Caterpillar-Caterpillar" from *When I Was a Child* by Anna Moo (Anna Moo Good Moo's Productions)

Someday, Fuzzy Caterpillar

Materials

none

Use the Fuzzy Caterpillar Stick Puppet to recite the following poem:
> *Fuzzy, fuzzy caterpillar*
> *Creeping, crawling by.*
> *Don't you know that someday*
> *You will be a butterfly?*
> *Don't you know that someday*
> *You will be a butterfly?*

Invite children to tell the puppet what they might like to be someday.

The Metamorphosis

Materials

The Very Hungry Caterpillar by Eric Carle
scissors
felt (assorted colors)
plastic sheet protector
glue gun
Velcro
felt board

Cut felt to resemble the food items in *The Very Hungry Caterpillar.* Cut a pair of wings from a plastic sheet protector, and glue a piece of Velcro to each wing. Read the story aloud. Have the Fuzzy Caterpillar Stick Puppet retell the story of the hungry caterpillar's metamorphosis. Put the felt cutouts on a felt board, and use the puppet to remove each item as it is "eaten" by the caterpillar in the story. At the part where the butterfly emerges from the cocoon, add wings to the puppet to change it into a butterfly. To extend the activity, encourage children to use the puppet to retell the story to each other.

Turtle Sock Puppet

Materials

Mouth pattern (page 126)
scissors
men's green athletic sock
cardboard
glue gun
wiggly eyes
dark-green and light-green felt

Directions

Cut off the end of the sock. Make a copy of the Mouth pattern, and cut it out. Trace the pattern onto cardboard, cut it out, and fold it in half. Glue the cardboard to the end of the sock to create a mouth. Glue on wiggly eyes. Cut out two 10" (25.5 cm) squares from dark-green felt, and round the edges. Glue two opposing sides from each felt piece to form a "tunnel." Cut four legs from light-green felt, and glue them along the bottom of the "shell." Decorate the shell with light-green felt scraps. Place your hand inside the sock, and slide it through the shell.

Variation

Use red felt and add a stem and leaves cut from construction paper to create an apple. The sock will be the worm puppet that lives in the apple.

Reading Recommendations

Franklin Goes to School by Paulette Bourgeois
A House is a House for Me by Mary Ann Hoberman
I Wish I Could Fly by Ron Maris
The Tortoise and the Hare by Betty Miles
Yertle the Turtle by Dr. Seuss

Song Suggestions

"A House is a House for Me" from *A House is a House* by Fred Penner (Youngheart Music)
"The Little Turtle" from *A Twinkle in Your Eye* by Burl Ives (Sony Music Entertainment)

Listening and Speaking Skills

The Shy Guy

Materials

none

Tell children that the Turtle Sock Puppet is very shy when the class is noisy. Explain to children that the puppet will only come out when they are quiet. When the class is quiet, push out the turtle's head, and recite the following poem:

T-u-r t-l-e.
Turtle is as slow as can be.
He never goes too far away.
He takes his house along each day.
T-u-r t-l-e
Won't you be a friend to me?

Places to Put a Turtle

Materials

none

Use the Turtle Sock Puppet to teach children the poem below. Encourage children to pantomime the words as they chant.

I had a little turtle.
*I put him **in a box.***
He swam in a puddle.
He climbed on the rocks.
He snapped at a minnow.
He snapped at a flea.
He snapped at a mosquito.
And he snapped at me.
He caught the minnow.
He caught the flea.
He caught the mosquito.
But he didn't catch me!

Ask children to name other places they might put a turtle. Encourage children to think of words that rhyme with this place. Use children's ideas to change the boldfaced words to create a new poem.

Listening and Speaking Skills

Spider Glove Puppet

Materials
scissors
pair of men's dark-colored garden gloves
needle and black or brown thread (optional)
glue gun
black yarn
small index card
wiggly eyes

Directions
Cut three fingers from one glove, and stitch or glue them to the second glove (creating eight "legs"). Use black yarn and an index card to make a pom-pom ball spider head. Cut a 10" (25.5 cm) piece of yarn, and set it aside. Wrap the remaining yarn around the length of a small index card. (The more yarn you use the fuller the pom-pom ball will be.) Slide the yarn off the card, and tightly tie the 10" piece around the middle. Cut both ends of the bundle, and fluff the yarn to create a pom-pom ball. Glue the pom-pom ball to the top of the glove, and glue wiggly eyes to the pom-pom ball.

• •

Variation
Use gray gloves and omit the yarn pom-pom ball to create an octopus puppet.

Reading Recommendations
Anansi the Spider: A Tale from the Ashanti by Gerald McDermott
The Itsy Bitsy Spider by Iza Trapani
Miss Spider's Tea Party by David Kirk
Spiders, Spiders Everywhere! by Rozanne Lanczak Williams (Creative Teaching Press)
The Very Busy Spider by Eric Carle

Song Suggestions
"Anansi" and "Spider on the Floor" from *The Singable Songs Collection* by Raffi (Rounder Records)
"The Eensy Weensy Spider" from *Great Big Hits* by Sharon, Lois, and Bram (Drive)
"Hey, Mr. Spider" from *Make Believe* by Linda Arnold (Youngheart Music)
"Itsy Bitsy Spider" from *Big Fun* by Greg & Steve (Youngheart Music)
"Spider Dan" from *Pictures on the Fridge* by Norman Foote (Youngheart Music)

Spider Songs

Materials

none

Use the Spider Glove Puppet to lead the class in a round of "Itsy Bitsy Spider." Encourage children to use a different voice, such as that of a great big daddy spider, mommy spider, or baby spider, to sing the song with the puppet.

Eight Great Legs

Materials

drawing paper
crayons or markers

Use the Spider Glove Puppet to lead a discussion about what a person would be able to do if he or she had a combination of eight arms and legs. Ask children to illustrate on drawing paper what they could do if they had a combination of eight arms and legs. Encourage children to present their work to their classmates.

Listening and Speaking Skills

Owl Mitten Puppet

Materials
   scissors
   pair of mittens
   glue gun
   felt (assorted colors)
   wiggly eyes

Directions
Cut off the thumb of a mitten. Make a small slit in another mitten opposite the thumb that is already there and glue the cut thumb over it to create hands for the puppet. Cut out felt ears, large eyes, eyebrows, and a beak, and glue them to the puppet. Glue on wiggly eyes over the felt eyes.

• •

Variation
Add wiggly eyes, a beak cut from yellow felt, wings cut from black felt, and a white felt circle for a tummy to a black mitten to create a penguin puppet.

Reading Recommendations
   Owl at Home by Arnold Lobel
   Owl Moon by Jane Yolen
   Owly by Mike Thaler
   The Sleepy Owl by Marcus Pfister

Song Suggestions
   "Owl Lullaby" from *Sing A to Z* by Sharon, Lois, and Bram (A&M Records)

What a Hoot!

Materials

index cards

Have the Owl Mitten Puppet invite children to make the sound an owl makes. Then, ask children to name other words they know that have the same /oo/ sound, such as *hoot, tool,* and *spoon.* Write these words on index cards, and display them on a word wall. Have the class read the words along with the puppet. Encourage children to read the words as an owl would, with an emphasis on the /oo/.

Whoo's Ready?

Materials

none

Use the Owl Mitten Puppet to capture children's attention before you read them a story. Have the puppet ask *Whoo... who is ready for a story? Whoo... who is sitting quietly?* Have the puppet praise children who are ready to listen. For example, say *Madison, I like the way you are sitting very quietly* or *I see you all are ready for a story!*

Listening and Speaking Skills

Splatter-Shield Mask

Materials
- scissors
- felt (assorted colors)
- glue gun
- large kitchen splatter shield
- art supplies (e.g., yarn, buttons, ribbon, fabric)

Directions
Cut eyes, eyebrows, a nose, and a mouth from felt, and glue them onto the splatter shield. Use art supplies to personalize the puppet.

Variation
Use art supplies to transform a pair of splatter shields into popular characters, such as Jack and Jill, Hansel and Gretel, or Beauty and the Beast.

Reading Recommendations
Jambo Means Hello by Muriel Feelings
People Say Hello by Will Barber (Creative Teaching Press)
Richard Scarry's Please and Thank You Book by Richard Scarry

Song Suggestions
"Jambo" and "Greetings in Many Languages" from *Multicultural Children's Songs* by Ella Jenkins (Folkways/Smithsonian)

Thank You for Saying Please

Materials

Richard Scarry's Please and Thank You Book by Richard Scarry

Create two Splatter-Shield Masks that are decorated differently, and use them to help children practice their manners. Read aloud scenarios from *Richard Scarry's Please and Thank You Book* in which the characters say *please* and *thank you*. Use the puppets to act out the scenes. Encourage children to discuss the puppets' dialogue, and invite children to use the puppets during a free-choice period to practice these "magic" words.

Learning a Language

Materials

none

Create a boy and a girl Splatter-Shield Mask to use in bilingual activities. Have one puppet speak English and the other puppet speak another language. Invite children to ask the puppets questions. Have each puppet respond in his or her respective language. Encourage children to use the puppets during a free-choice period to practice their own foreign and native language skills. Children are less likely to be embarrassed by mistakes because the puppet is doing all of the talking!

Wiggle Worm Puppet

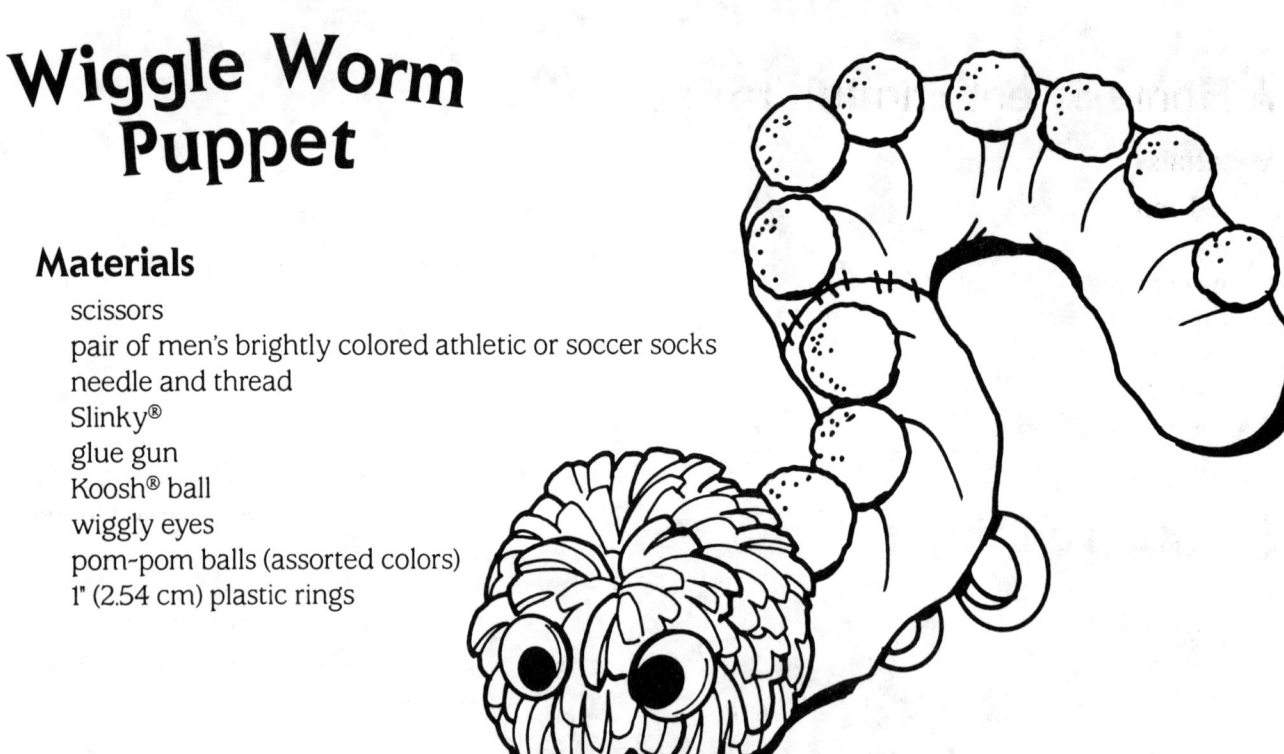

Materials
scissors
pair of men's brightly colored athletic or soccer socks
needle and thread
Slinky®
glue gun
Koosh® ball
wiggly eyes
pom-pom balls (assorted colors)
1" (2.54 cm) plastic rings

Directions
Cut off the toe from the pair of socks. Turn the socks so that the fuzzy side faces out. Partially insert one sock into the other sock to create one long sock, and stitch them together where they overlap. Insert a Slinky® through the socks, and stitch it to both ends. Glue a Koosh® ball to one end of the puppet, and glue wiggly eyes to it. Glue small, colorful pom-pom balls to the top of the sock. Sew plastic rings along the bottom of the sock, and place your fingers through them to move the puppet.

• •

Variation
Omit the pom-pom balls, and glue wiggly eyes directly onto the sock. Glue a cardboard mouth to the cut end of the sock and the Koosh® ball to the opposite end to create a rattlesnake puppet.

Reading Recommendations
Inch by Inch by Leo Lionni
Who Lives Here? by Rozanne Lanczak Williams (Creative Teaching Press)
Worms Wiggle by David Pelham

Song Suggestions
"Shake My Sillies Out" from *The Singable Songs Collection* by Raffi (Rounder Records)
"Ten Wiggle Worms (Parts I and II)" from *"So Big": Activity Songs for Little Ones* by Hap Palmer (Hap Palmer Recordings)
"Walter the Waltzing Worm" from *Walter the Waltzing Worm* by Hap Palmer (Educational Activities, Inc.)
"Wiggle in My Toe" from *Late Last Night* by Joe Scruggs (Lyrick Studios)
"Wiggle Wobble" from *We All Live Together, Volume 1* by Greg & Steve (Youngheart Music)

A Home Sweet Enough to Eat

Materials
red apple
rock
watering can
ruler
twig
knife

Invite a child to help you use the Wiggle Worm Puppet, a red apple, a rock, a watering can, a ruler for a fence, and a twig for a tree to tell the class a story. Ask the child to raise each prop that is named in the story, and move the puppet as you tell the following story.

A little worm was looking for a house that had no door or window, but a star inside. The little worm looked and looked. He looked under a rock. He looked inside a watering can. He looked behind a fence. Then he looked up a tree. There it was—a red house without a door or a window (hold up the apple, then cut it in half to reveal a "star"), *but a star inside!*

Wiggling into a Good Story

Materials
"Shake My Sillies Out" by Raffi
CD/cassette player

Use the Wiggle Worm Puppet to help children review good manners for listening to a story, such as sitting quietly and keeping their hands and feet still. Invite children to "get rid of their wiggles." Play "Shake My Sillies Out," and ask children to follow the directions in the song. Then, say *Now that your wiggles are gone, we can all sit quietly for a story.*

Listening and Speaking Skills

Pee-Wee, the Ping-Pong Paddle Puppet

Materials
scissors
black and red felt
glue gun
Ping-Pong balls and paddle
pom-pom ball

Directions
Cut two ½" (13 mm) circles from black felt, and glue them to two Ping-Pong balls to create eyes. Glue the eyes onto a Ping-Pong paddle. Glue on a pom-pom ball for a nose. Cut a mouth from red felt, and glue it below the nose.

●●●

Variation
Cut four 1" (2.5 cm) strips of paper, and fold them accordion-style to make arms and legs. Cut hands and feet from construction paper, and glue one to the end of each strip. Glue the arms and legs and a bow tie cut from construction paper to the Pee-Wee, the Ping-Pong Paddle Puppet to create a Humpty Dumpty puppet.

Reading Recommendations
Animal Shapes by Brian Wildsmith
Color Farm by Lois Ehlert
I See Shapes by Marcia Fries (Creative Teaching Press)
Mr. Brown Can Moo, Can You? by Dr. Seuss
Shapes, Shapes, Shapes by Tana Hoban

Song Suggestions
"Round in a Circle" from *We All Live Together, Volume 1* by Greg & Steve (Youngheart Music)

Ping, Pong, Sing Me a Song

Materials
attribute blocks

Place an assortment of attribute blocks before each child or pairs of children. Allow children time to determine which shapes are in their pile. Then, use Pee-Wee to lead children in singing this version of "Rain, Rain, Go Away." Encourage children to find the shape named in the song.

Up, down,
All around.
Look at all the shapes
We've found.

Ping, pong,
Sing along.
*Hold up a **square***
As we sing our song.

Change the boldfaced word to the name of another shape, and repeat the activity.

That Looks Familiar

Materials
none

Invite children to sit in a circle. Hold Pee-Wee to your face. Look around the room for an object with an obvious shape (e.g., clock, door, desk), and say *Look! See! Look! I see something square.* Invite children to name the square object you have in sight. Hand the puppet to the child sitting next to you, and ask him or her to repeat the process.

Shapes

Sergeant Shape Puppet

Materials

Body pattern (page 128)
Sergeant Shape pattern (page 129)
scissors
felt (assorted colors)
needle and thread (optional)
glue gun
wiggly eyes
yarn
marker
Velcro

Directions

Make a copy of the Body pattern, and cut it out. Place two pieces of felt together, and trace the pattern on the top piece. Cut out both shapes. Stitch or glue them together, leaving the bottom edge open. Glue wiggly eyes on the face and yarn hair to the back side of the puppet. Use a marker to draw other facial features. Make a copy of the Sergeant Shape pattern, and cut out the pieces. Trace the buttons, stripes, pentagon, and star onto felt; cut them out; and glue Velcro to each piece. Glue Velcro to the places that the buttons, stripes, pentagon, and star should go on the sergeant's uniform, and attach the felt pieces.

Variation

Change the puppet's uniform to that of another community helper, such as a police officer, letter carrier, or firefighter.

Reading Recommendations

Color Zoo by Lois Ehlert
Shapes by Paul Yenawine
Shapes, Shapes, Shapes by Tana Hoban

Song Suggestions

"Shapes" from *We All Live Together, Volume 3* by Greg & Steve (Youngheart Music)

Shaping Up

Materials

none

Organize the class into small groups. Have Sergeant Shape direct groups to work together to make different shapes with their bodies. Encourage children to find creative ways to form circles, rectangles, and other geometric figures. Have the puppet compliment children who are working well together.

In Good Shape

Materials

none

Display Sergeant Shape, and invite individual children to remove the shape named in the following couplet:
Lucas, stand and take a bow.
Please take a **star** from the Sergeant now.

Change the boldfaced words to a new child's name and a different shape. Repeat the activity, and play until there are no shapes remaining on the puppet.

Shapes

Clown Bottle Puppet

Materials
Clown pattern (page 130)
Bottle Body pattern (page 131)
scissors
felt (assorted colors)
scissors
needle and thread (optional)
glue gun
rubber band
empty plastic 32 oz. (946 mL) liquid detergent bottle
Velcro

Directions
Make a copy of the Clown pattern and the Bottle Body pattern, and cut out the pieces. Place two pieces of felt together, and trace the Bottle Body pattern on the top piece. Cut out both shapes, and stitch or glue them together, leaving the top and bottom edges open. Use glue and a rubber band to attach the body to the opening of an empty detergent bottle. Trace the facial features and hands on felt, cut them out, and glue Velcro to each piece. Attach the facial features and hands to the puppet.

•••

Variation
Use art supplies to create different characters, such as a princess, ringmaster, nurse, or pirate.

Reading Recommendations
Arthur's Birthday by Marc Brown
Bear in a Square by Stella Blackstone
Circles, Triangles, and Squares by Tana Hoban
The Secret Birthday Message by Eric Carle
There's a Square by Mary Serfozo
Where a Line Bends . . . a Shape Begins by Rhonda Gowler Greene

Song Suggestions
"Clover the Clown" and "Crazy Clowns" from *Circus Magic: Under the Big Top* by Linda Arnold (Youngheart Music)
"Happy Birthday" from *Happy Birthday* by Sharon, Lois, and Bram (A&M Records)

Clowning around with Shapes

Materials
none

Remove the shapes from the Clown Bottle Puppet, and make them accessible to the class. Invite a child to add the body part named in the following couplet:

This poor little clown wants you to replace
*The **nose** that is missing from his face.*

Invite another child to participate. Change the boldfaced word to a different facial feature, and repeat the activity until the puppet is dressed with a happy face!

The Birthday Clown's Secret Message

Materials
The Secret Birthday Message by Eric Carle
scissors
construction paper (assorted colors)
resealable plastic bag

Use this activity to celebrate the birthday of each child born in a given month. Invite children to stand before the class, and have the Clown Bottle Puppet lead the class in singing "Happy Birthday" to them. Then, read aloud *The Secret Birthday Message*. Cut from various colors of construction paper the shapes from the story (i.e., semicircle, star, oval, triangle, circle, "stairs," square, and rectangle), place them in a resealable plastic bag, and place the bag and a copy of the book at the math center. Encourage children to use the shape cutouts to retell the story or make their own "secret" messages.

Shapes

Fish Stick Puppet

Materials

Fish pattern (page 132)
scissors
cardboard
felt (assorted colors)
glue gun
tongue depressor
art supplies (e.g., markers, puff paint, sequins)

Directions

Make a copy of the Fish pattern, and cut it out. Trace the pattern on cardboard, and cut it out. Place two small pieces of felt together, trace the Fish pattern on the top piece, and cut out both fish shapes. Glue a tongue depressor to the bottom of the cardboard. Glue one felt fish shape to each side of the cardboard. Use art supplies to decorate the puppet.

Variation

Create other shape patterns, such as a sun, a moon, stars, and planets, to affix to tongue depressors to create astronomy puppets.

Reading Recommendations

Fish Eyes by Lois Ehlert
Fishes by Brian Wildsmith
One Fish, Two Fish, Red Fish, Blue Fish by Dr. Seuss
Swimmy by Leo Lionni

Song Suggestions

"Five Little Fishies" from *Sing A to Z* by Sharon, Lois, and Bram (A&M Records)
"Three Little Fishes" from *Mainly Mother Goose* by Sharon, Lois, and Bram (Drive)

Follow Me, Fish

Materials
none

In advance, make a yellow, red, blue, or green Fish Stick Puppet for each child. Give each child a puppet, and tell children to follow the directions given when their color is named. For example, say *All red fish swim to the door*, *All blue fish swim to the teacher*, or *All green fish swim to the window*.

Swimmy

Materials
Swimmy by Leo Lionni

In advance, create several red and one black Fish Stick Puppets. Arrange children in a circle, and give each one a puppet to help you tell the story of *Swimmy*. Invite children to use the puppets to pantomime the actions in the story as you read it aloud. After the activity, collect the red puppets. Invite the child who is holding the black puppet to share something that makes him or her different but special. Have the child pass the black puppet to the child sitting next to him or her, and encourage that child to share something about him or herself. Repeat the process until each child has handled the black puppet.

Turkey Glove Puppet

Materials
Turkey and Feather patterns (page 133)
scissors
red, orange, green, blue, and brown felt
needle and thread (optional)
glue gun
men's brown garden glove

Directions
Make a copy of the Turkey and Feather patterns, and cut them out. Use the feather pattern to trace eight feathers on red, orange, green, and blue felt. (Make two of each color.) Cut out the feathers, stitch or glue together the edges of each pair, leaving the bottom edge open, and slip one over each finger of the glove. Use the turkey pattern to trace two heads on a piece of brown felt. Cut out the heads, and stitch or glue the top and left edges together, leaving the back and bottom edges open. Glue the turkey's head to the thumb of the glove.

Variation
Trace the turkey pattern on blue felt, and cut off the wattle. Glue the head and colorful feathers to a work glove that has been dyed blue to create a peacock puppet.

Reading Recommendations
Celebrating Thanksgiving: Giving Thanks by Joel Kupperstein (Creative Teaching Press)
Is It Red? Is It Yellow? or Is It Blue? by Tana Hoban
Little Blue and Little Yellow by Leo Lionni
Oh, What a Thanksgiving! by Steven Kroll
A Turkey for Thanksgiving by Eve Bunting

Song Suggestions
"Rainbow of Colors" from *We All Live Together, Volume 5* by Greg & Steve (Youngheart Music)
"Turkey in the Straw" from *Sing Along Stew* by Linda Arnold (Youngheart Music)

Parade of Colors

Materials

colored markers
chart paper

Display the Turkey Glove Puppet, and say *No two colors are the same. How many **red** things can you name?* Ask children to name things that are red (e.g., strawberries, apples, hearts), and use a red marker to write their ideas on chart paper. Change the boldfaced word to *orange, green,* or *blue.* Repeat the process using the colored marker that matches the color named in the verse and a new piece of chart paper. Display these charts on a wall. To extend the activity, ask each child to choose an item from a list to illustrate. Invite children to line up with their picture. Use the puppet to lead children in a parade around the room or school as they cheer *Red, orange, green, and blue. Without colors, what would we do?*

Giving Thanks

Materials

none

Each day, invite a different child to share with the class some things for which he or she is grateful. Invite the child to stand before the class, and place the Turkey Glove Puppet on his or her hand. Encourage the child to point to the first feather on the turkey's back and name something for which he or she is thankful (e.g., *I am thankful for my sister*). Ask the child to repeat the process with the three remaining feathers. Encourage children to clap for their classmate after the presentation.

Perry Parrot Sock Puppet

Materials
cup
fuzzy ankle sock
marker
glue gun
wiggly eyes
pom-pom balls
scissors
yellow felt
multicolored craft feathers

Directions
Insert a cup into the sock, decide where to place a set of eyes, and make a dot for each eye with a marker. Glue a pair of wiggly eyes onto a pair of pom-pom balls, and glue the pom-pom balls to the dots on the sock. Cut a large beak from a piece of yellow felt, and glue it under the eyes. Glue feathers behind the eyes and down the back of the puppet. Remove the cup, and place your hand inside the sock to manipulate the puppet.

●●

Variation
Place black feathers down the back of a white sock to create a bald eagle puppet

Reading Recommendations
Cat's Colors by Jan Cabrera
Color Dance by Ann Jonas
The Color Wizard by Barbara Brenner
Growing Colors by Bruce McMillan
I See Colors by Rozanne Lanczak Williams (Creative Teaching Press)

Song Suggestions
"Parade of Colors" and "Put a Little Color on You" from *Can a Cherry Pie Wave Goodbye?*
    by Hap Palmer (Hap Palmer Recordings)
"Percival the Parrot" from *Sally the Swinging Snake* by Hap Palmer (Educational Activities, Inc.)

Color Code

Materials

none

Invite children to stand in a circle. Stand in the middle of the circle with Perry Parrot. Tell children to follow the directions Perry Parrot gives them in the following couplet: *Feathers of **blue** cover Perry Parrot. Please sit down if today you also wear it.*

Change the boldfaced word to a different color, and repeat the chant until each child is seated again.

Birds of a Feather

Materials

multicolored craft feathers

Encourage children to use feathers to create colorful patterns or sort them into groups. As children work, use Perry Parrot to make comments about what they are doing, such as *I think your pattern is red, red, blue* or *You have collected all of the yellow feathers.*

Colors

Flip and Flop Kitchen Sponge Puppets

Materials

glue gun
pom-pom balls
2 small kitchen dish-scrubber
    brushes or sponges
2 pieces of ribbon
    (2 different colors)

Directions

Glue pom-pom balls for eyes and a nose to a kitchen dish-scrubber brush or sponge. Create two matching puppets. Tie a different colored piece of ribbon around the neck of each puppet.

Variation

Dip the top of a kitchen dish-scrubber brush in green paint and the handle in brown paint to create a tree. Allow the paint to dry. Tape small apples, coconuts, or letters cut from construction paper to the tree puppet, and use the puppet to accompany a reading of *The Giving Tree* by Shel Silverstein or *Chicka Chicka Boom Boom* by Bill Martin Jr. and John Archambault.

Reading Recommendations

Becca Backward, Becca Forward by Bruce McMillan
Exactly the Opposite by Tana Hoban
Opposites by Demi
Opposites by Rosalind Kightley
Push, Pull, Empty, Full by Tana Hoban
Spot Looks at Opposites by Eric Hill
Would You Rather Be a Bullfrog? by Dr. Seuss

Song Suggestions

"The Opposite" from *Make Believe* by Linda Arnold (Youngheart Music)
"Say the Opposite" from *Can a Cherry Pie Wave Goodbye?* by Hap Palmer
    (Hap Palmer Recordings)

A Name Change

Materials

marker
chart paper

Use a marker to write the words *Flip* and *Flop* on chart paper. Ask children to explain what makes the names of Flip and Flop alike and different. Prompt children to say that both words start with /fl/. Invite children to name other words that start with /fl/, and write their ideas on the chart paper. To give the children more practice with sound manipulation, encourage them to substitute the beginning (e.g., *Chip* and *Chop* or *Tip* and *Top*) or ending sounds (e.g., *Flit* and *Flot* or *Flick* and *Flock*) to create new names for the puppets.

In, Out, Whisper, Shout

Materials

none

Use Flip and Flop to introduce opposites. For example, tell children that Flip is *up* and Flop is *down*. Ask children to tell Flip things that are up in the sky and tell Flop things that are found down on the ground. Change the pair of opposites, and repeat the activity. For example, choose the words *over* and *under*, and have children tell Flip and Flop things they can climb over or under.

Alike and Different

Wooden Spoon and Fork Puppets

Materials

glue gun
wiggly eyes
wooden spoon and fork
scissors
felt (assorted colors)
yarn

Directions

Glue a pair of wiggly eyes to a wooden spoon and a wooden fork. Cut out from felt other facial features (e.g., eyes, a nose, and a mouth), and glue them onto the spoon and fork. Use glue to attach yarn for hair.

Variation

Draw a face on the wooden spoon. Glue a hat, arms, and bib overalls cut from felt to the wooden spoon to create a farmer puppet. Glue the wooden fork to the farmer's arm for use as a pitchfork.

Reading Recommendations

Gregory, the Terrible Eater by Mitchell Sharmat
Today is Monday by Eric Carle
What's for Lunch? by Eric Carle
Yummies by James Marshall

Song Suggestions

"Home-Made Cooking" from *Jumpin' Jack* by Jack Grunsky (Youngheart Music)
"On Top of Spaghetti" from *Jeremiah Was a Bullfrog!* by Hoyt Axton (Youngheart Music)
"The Vegetable Lament" from *Make Believe* by Linda Arnold (Youngheart Music)

Opposite Objects

Materials
pairs of objects (e.g., boot/gym shoe, baseball cap/firefighter helmet, encyclopedia/storybook)

Show children the Wooden Spoon and Fork Puppets. Ask children to describe how they are alike and different. Show children another pair of objects that have obvious similarities and differences. Ask children to discuss with the puppets what the objects in each pair have in common and what makes them different.

Good and Good for You

Materials
scissors
magazines
tape
poster board

In advance, cut out magazine pictures of healthy food and junk food. Try to find pictures of related foods. For example, cut out pictures of a baked potato and french fries, applesauce and a caramel apple, or a bagel and a doughnut. Tape one picture from each pair of foods to each puppet. Ask students to explain how the foods in the pictures are alike and different. Ask children to name which of the two foods is healthier for our bodies. To extend learning, give each child a food picture. Invite children to decide whether to tape their picture to a poster titled *Healthy Food* or one titled *Junk Food*. After the activity, display posters as a reminder to children to eat healthy!

Alike and Different

Flower Finger Puppets

Materials

Garden pattern (page 134)
scissors
felt (assorted colors)
glue gun
Velcro
art supplies (e.g., glitter, puff paint)
men's white or green garden glove

Directions

Make a copy of the Garden pattern. Cut out the flowers (do not use the vegetables for this puppet), and trace each one onto a piece of felt. Cut out the felt flowers, and glue a piece of Velcro to the back of each one. Use art supplies to decorate the flowers. Glue a piece of Velcro to each finger of the glove, and attach each flower.

Variation

Attach different holiday shapes and symbols (e.g., pumpkins, hearts, shamrocks) to the fingers of the glove for use with festive songs and fingerplays.

Reading Recommendations

Chrysanthemum by Kevin Henkes
Ferdinand the Bull by Munro Leaf
Planting Flowers by Lois Ehlert
Spot in the Garden by Eric Hill

Song Suggestions

"Being Different's OK with Me" from *Anna Banana* by Kathleen Gibson (Rompin' Records)
"Grandmother's Garden" from *I'm a Can-Do Kid* by John Archambault and David Plummer (Creative Teaching Press)

A Story to Grow On

Materials

Ferdinand the Bull by Munro Leaf

Display the Flower Finger Puppets as you read aloud *Ferdinand the Bull*. Discuss with children what made Ferdinand different from the other bulls. Ask children to use the puppets to share five things about themselves that make them different from other people.

Growing up Together in Different Ways

Materials

none

Show children the Flower Finger Puppets, and ask them to name ways the flowers are alike and different. Discuss with children ways people are alike and different. Have children suggest ways of getting along with all types of people, such as being considerate and friendly.

Alike and Different

Elephant Sock Puppet

Materials

Elephant pattern (page 135)
gray tagboard
scissors
duct tape
men's gray athletic sock
empty toilet-paper tubes
glue gun
large wiggly eyes

Directions

Make a copy of the Elephant pattern. Enlarge the pattern on gray tagboard, and cut it out. Score the ears, and bend them forward. Place a piece of duct tape along the place on the back side where each ear is folded to provide support. Cut out a hole for a nose that is slightly smaller than the width of the sock. Slide two empty toilet-paper tubes into the sock, and insert the sock through the hole in the tagboard. Glue a pair of large wiggly eyes above the trunk. Hold the elephant's head in one hand, and insert the other hand into the sock to move the trunk.

●●●

Variation

Cut a long, thin face with small ears from light-brown tagboard, and glue on large wiggly eyes. Insert a light-brown sock through the hole to create an aardvark puppet.

Reading Recommendations

Bashi, the Elephant Baby by Theresa Radcliffe
The Polite Elephant by Richard Scarry
Right Number of Elephants by Jeff Sheppard

Song Suggestions

"One Elephant" from *Great Big Hits* by Sharon, Lois, and Bram (Drive)
"Push the Elephant" from *Nora's Room* by Jessica Harper (Alcazar)

The Enormous Elephant

Materials
felt numbers/felt board or magnetic numbers/magnetic board

Distribute a felt or magnetic number to each child. Recite the chant below. For each verse, have all children with that number "feed" it to the Elephant Sock Puppet and then place it on the felt or magnetic board.

*One enormous elephant was having lots of fun.
He was oh so silly when he ate number 1.*

*One enormous elephant didn't know what to do.
He was so very shy when he ate number 2.*

*One enormous elephant sitting beneath a tree
Almost fell asleep when he ate number 3.*

*One enormous elephant felt rather poor.
His big tummy growled as he ate number 4.*

*One enormous elephant feeling so alive,
Trumpeted his trunk as he ate number 5.*

*One enormous elephant doing silly tricks,
Hopped up and down as he ate number 6.*

*One enormous elephant looked up at heaven.
"Thank you," he said, as he ate number 7.*

*One enormous elephant was worried he'd be late.
He rushed and he hurried and he ate number 8.*

*One enormous elephant really loved to dine.
He sat right down and ate number 9.*

*One enormous elephant ate number 10.
Excitedly he said, "Let's do it all again!"*

Numbers

Peter Pointer Sleeve Puppet

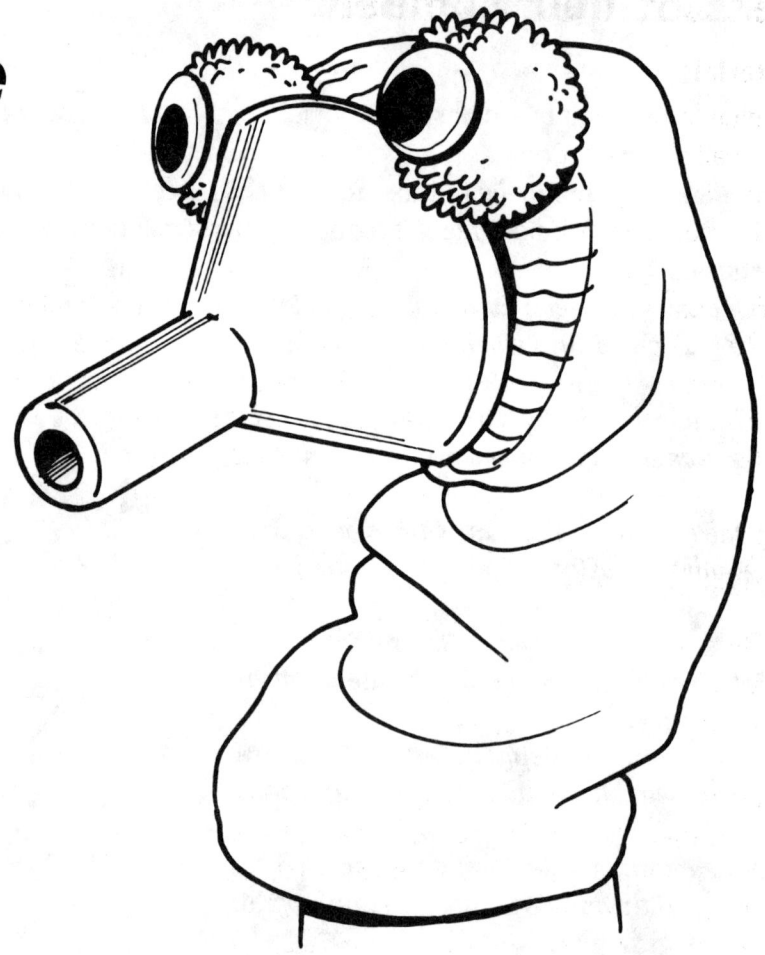

Materials
scissors
men's long-sleeved T-shirt
funnel
glue gun
large wiggly eyes
large pom-pom balls

Directions
Cut off one sleeve from the T-shirt. Insert a funnel through the cuffed end, and glue it in place. Glue large wiggly eyes onto two large pom-pom balls, and glue the pom-pom balls above the funnel for eyes.

• •

Variation
Add feathers to create a woodpecker puppet.

Reading Recommendations
Anno's Counting Book by Mitsumasa Anno
I See Patterns by Linda Benton
Who Took the Cookies from the Cookie Jar? by Rozanne Lanczak Williams
   (Creative Teaching Press)
Who's Counting? by Nancy Tafuri

Song Suggestions
"1, 2, Buckle My Shoe" from *We All Live Together, Volume 3* by Greg & Steve (Youngheart Music)
"Counting Kittens" from *Counting Kittens* by John Archambault and David Plummer
   (Creative Teaching Press)

He's Got Your Number

Materials

glue
small square gift box
marker
felt numbers/felt board or magnetic numbers/magnetic board

Glue a small square gift box shut. Use a marker to print a number on each side to make a die. Display a felt or magnetic board, and give each child a felt or magnetic number. Roll the die. Have Peter Pointer "look" at the die, and say *Peter Pointer, look and see. What is the number that you have for me?* Announce the number on the die, and have all children with that number come up and place it on the felt or magnetic board.

Point It Out

Materials

paper
crayons or markers

Assign each child a number (e.g., 2 or 4) and the name of an object (e.g., sandwich or pear). Invite children to draw that number of their object (e.g., two sandwiches or four pears). Display children's work in random order around the room. Invite individual children to use Peter Pointer to point to the picture that shows a particular quantity that you name. For example, say *Point to the picture of eight butterflies* or *Which picture shows one elephant?* Continue the activity until each child has had an opportunity to manipulate the puppet and identify a quantity.

Numbers 57

Bunny Finger Puppets

Materials
scissors
white cotton work glove
glue gun
wiggly eyes
pink pom-pom balls
marker
white felt

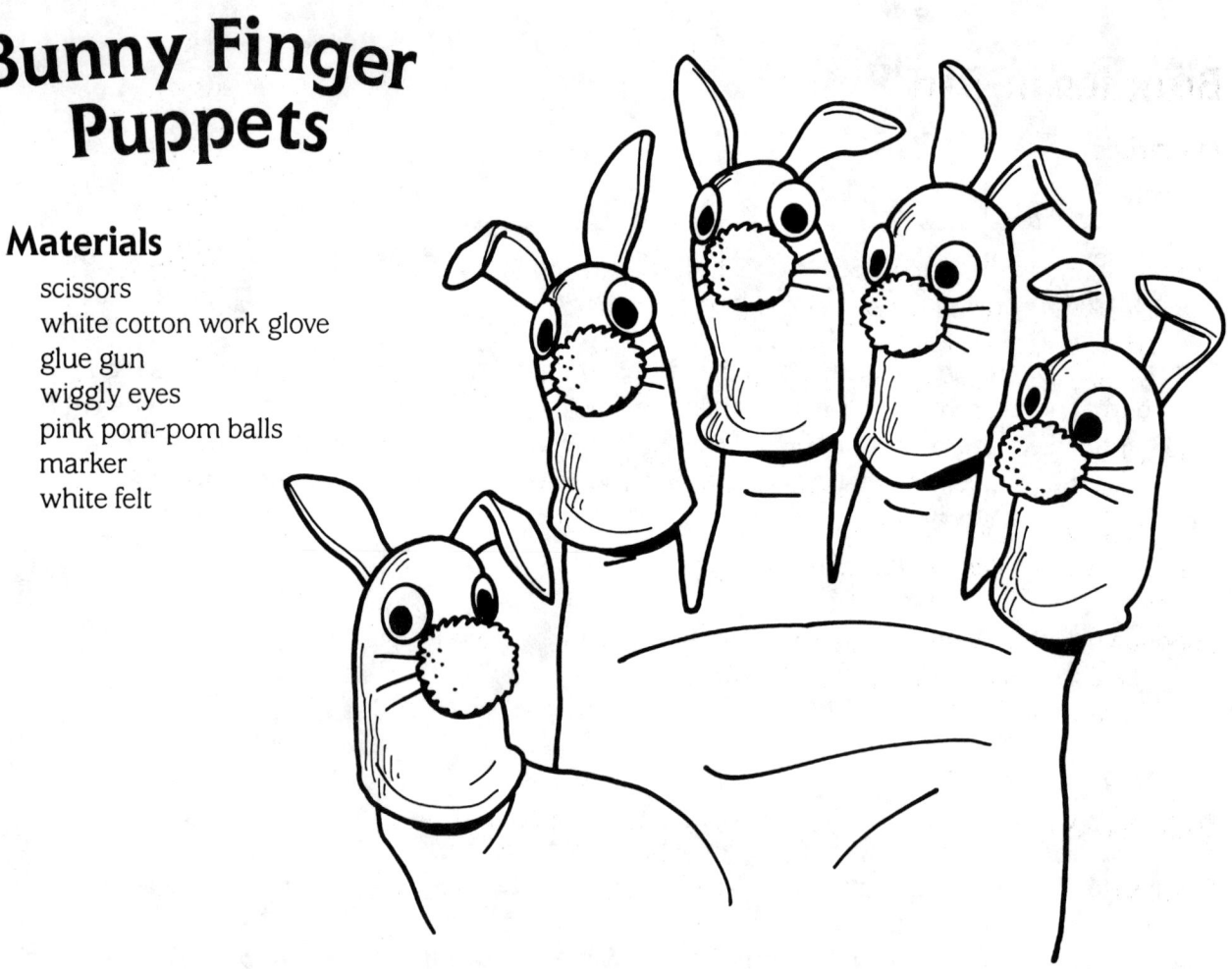

Directions
Cut off the fingers from the glove. Glue a pair of wiggly eyes and a pink pom-pom ball for a nose to each finger. Use a marker to draw whiskers beside each nose. Cut ears from white felt, and glue them above each face.

• •

Variation
Use a gray glove and small ears cut from gray felt to create mice puppets.

Reading Recommendations
Little Bunny's Sleepless Night by Carol Roth
Roll Over by M. Gerstein
The Tales of Peter Rabbit by Beatrix Potter
Ten in the Bed by Penny Dale
Ten, Nine, Eight by Molly Bang

Song Suggestions
"Number Exercise" from *The Best of Melody House, Volume 2* by Sharon Lucky (Melody House)
"Old John Rabbit" from *Mainly Mother Goose* by Sharon, Lois, and Bram (Drive)
"Ten in the Bed" from *Sing Along Stew* by Linda Arnold (Youngheart Music)

Bunnies in Bed

Materials
> none

Use the Bunny Finger Puppets to the lead class in singing or chanting
> There were **five** in the bed and the little one said,
> "Move over. Roll over!"
> So they all rolled over and one fell out.

Remove one puppet from your hand, and have the class sing
> There were **four** in the bed and the little one said,
> "Move over. Roll over!"
> So they all rolled over and one fell out.

Continue the process until only one bunny remains, and end the song with
> There was **one** in the bed and the little one said,
> "Good night!"

No More Bunnies Hopping on the Bed

Materials
> none

Use the Bunny Finger Puppets to lead children in singing a variation of "No More Monkeys Jumping on the Bed." Change the words to *No more bunnies **hopping** on the bed*, and encourage children to hop along as you sing the song!

Presto, the Pop-up Puppet

Materials

Body pattern (page 128)
wooden dowel or chopstick
small Styrofoam ball
scissors
fabric
glue gun
art supplies (e.g., markers, sequins, buttons)
sewing cone
wooden bead

Directions

Insert a wooden dowel or chopstick into a small Styrofoam ball. Make a copy of the Body pattern, and cut it out. Place two pieces of fabric together, trace the pattern on the top piece, and cut out both shapes. Glue the pieces together, leaving the top and bottom edges open. Glue the fabric "body" below the Styrofoam "head." Use art supplies to decorate the head and body. Insert the dowel or chopstick through the large side of a sewing cone and out the small side, and glue a wooden bead to the other end of the dowel or chopstick. Glue the bottom edge of the fabric around the large circle of the cone. Hold the dowel or chopstick with one hand and the cone with the other hand. To move the puppet, push the dowel or chopstick up and down.

●●

Variation

Glue a Styrofoam ball to the top of the cone. Glue facial features cut from craft foam to the Styrofoam ball to create an ice-cream-cone puppet.

Reading Recommendations

I Spy by Jean Marzollo
I Spy by Margaret Allen (Creative Teaching Press)

Song Suggestions

"Pop! Goes the Weasel" from *Great Big Hits* by Sharon, Lois, and Bram (Drive)
"Popcorn" from *We All Live Together, Volume 2* by Greg & Steve (Youngheart Music)

Pop Goes the Puppet!

Materials

simple instruments (e.g., xylophones, rhythm sticks, bongos)

Teach children the words to the following song:
Mr. Jack-in-the box,
All closed up tight.
Not a bit of air.
Not a bit of light.
Open the lid and out he pops!
That is the way with Jack-in-the-box!

Encourage children to use simple instruments to create a rhythm for the song. Ask children to sing as they play, and invite one child to manipulate Presto so that he emerges when the class sings the word *pops*.

Presto! It's Gone

Materials

various small objects (e.g., pencil, blocks, stapler)

Use Presto to lead this memory game. Place three to five small objects on a flat surface. Invite the class to gather around the objects, and ask them to identify what they see. Encourage children to examine the objects closely. Ask children to close their eyes. Remove one object from the table, and ask children to open their eyes again. Ask individual children to name the item that they think is missing. When the correct object is guessed, have the puppet pop up and say *Presto! You're right!* Place the object back on the table, and have the children play again.

Songs

Garden Man Coat-Hanger Puppet

Materials

Garden pattern (page 134)
wire coat hanger
glue gun
2 cardboard circles
2 white felt circles
scissors
felt (assorted colors)
Velcro

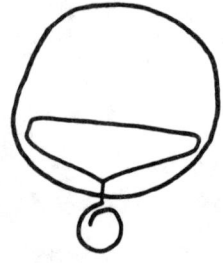

Directions

Untwist the handle of a wire coat hanger, and bend it into a circle. Twist the handle shut. Glue a cardboard circle the size of the hanger on the front and one on the back. Place glue on the edges of two white felt circles that match the size of the cardboard, and stick them to each piece of cardboard. Make one copy of the Garden pattern, and cut out the vegetables. (Do not use the flowers for this puppet.) Trace each vegetable onto a piece of felt, and cut out the pieces. Glue a piece of Velcro to the back of each vegetable, and arrange the pieces on one side of the hanger to create a face.

• •

Variation

Glue a piece of Velcro to a plastic spoon, and attach it to one side of the hanger. Place various felt letters on the hanger to create an alphabet soup puppet.

Reading Recommendations

Growing Vegetable Soup by Lois Ehlert
The Surprise Garden by Zoe Hall
The Tiny Seed by Eric Carle

Song Suggestions

"Aiken Drum" from *The Singable Songs Collection* by Raffi (Rounder Records)
"Stone Soup" from *Make Believe* by Linda Arnold (Youngheart Music)

Would You Like to Live in a Garden?

Materials
   none

Remove the facial features from the Garden Man Coat-Hanger Puppet. Hold up the felt-covered wire hanger, and invite children to sing this version of the song "Aiken Drum" to the puppet:

   A man lived in the garden,
   And he worked there all day long.
   His head was a big tortilla,
   As he worked there all day long.

Change the boldfaced words to a different part of the puppet's face (e.g., *His eyes were strawberries, His nose was an orange carrot, His mouth was a red tomato, His ears were brown potatoes*). Sing the new verse, and ask individual children to add to the puppet's face the vegetable facial feature that is named. Continue until the puppet's face is reassembled.

Look Who's Coming to Lunch

Materials
   none

"Invite" the Garden Man Coat-Hanger Puppet to lunch. Use the puppet to demonstrate and reinforce good table manners by having him say such things as *Please pass the salt* or *Thank you for chewing your food before you speak.*

Songs

Duck Car-Wash-Mitt Puppet

Materials
Mouth pattern (page 126)
scissors
felt
needle and thread
car-wash mitt
glue gun
wiggly eyes
ribbon

Directions
Make a copy of the Mouth pattern, and cut it out. Trace the pattern onto two pieces of felt, and cut them out. Cut one mouth piece in half widthwise, and position each half over the other felt mouth piece. Stitch or glue the rounded parts of the two halves to the other mouth piece. Make a slit widthwise in the middle of one side of the car-wash mitt. Fold the mouth in half, and insert the folded end through the slit. Stitch the top and bottom flaps of the mouth (the parts that are not folded) to the car-wash mitt. Glue two wiggly eyes above the bill. Tie a ribbon into a bow, and glue it above the cuff. Insert your fingers through the slit and into the mouth to manipulate the puppet.

●●●

Variation
Instead of a bill, glue on two ears and a nose cut from pink felt to create a sheep puppet.

Reading Recommendations
Come Along, Daisy! by Jane Simmons
Just You and Me by Sam McBratney
Make Way for Ducklings by Robert McCloskey
Scrawny, the Classroom Duck by S. Clymer
Ten Little Ducks by Franklin Hammond

Song Suggestions
"Little White Duck" from *Little White Duck* by Burl Ives (Columbia Records)
"Six Little Ducks" from *The Singable Songs Collection* by Raffi (Rounder Records)

Doin' a Ducky Dance

Materials

none

Use the Duck Car-Wash-Mitt Puppet to lead children in singing and playing a different version of "The Hokey Pokey." Arrange children in a circle, and invite them to sing and pantomime the following verse:

*You put your left **wing** in,*
*You take your left **wing** out.*
*You put your left **wing** in,*
And you shake it all about.
You do a ducky dance,
And then you turn yourself around.
That's what it's all about.

Change the boldfaced words to other parts of a duck's body, such as the *bill* or *tail feathers*, and have children continue singing, dancing, and having a "ducky" time.

You "Oughter" Be in Water

Materials

none

Invite children to join the Duck Car-Wash-Mitt Puppet in singing the following version of "Little White Duck":

There's a little white duck
Swimming in the water.
A little white duck who is
Doing what he oughter.

He said, "Come swim with me
Across the room and back.
You oughter follow me with a
Quack, quack, quack!"

Have the puppet lead a parade around the room or school. Invite the class to follow the duck and sing as they waddle along

Songs

Dog Stuffed-Animal Puppet

Materials
craft knife
dog stuffed animal
sock
needle and thread

Directions
Use a craft knife to cut along the back of a dog stuffed animal. Remove enough stuffing so that you can insert your hand inside. Place a sock over your hand, and insert it into the puppet. Stitch the sock along the edges where the sock and stuffed animal meet.

●●●

Variation
Follow the procedure using other stuffed animals to create more delightful puppets.

Reading Recommendations
Boomer's Big Surprise by Constance W. McGeorge
Cat and Dog by Rozanne Lanczak Williams (Creative Teaching Press)
Clifford, the Big Red Dog by Norman Bridwell
Oh Where, Oh Where Has My Little Dog Gone? by Iza Trapani
The Poky Little Puppy by Janette Sebring Lowrey

Song Suggestions
"B-I-N-G-O" from *The Best of Melody House, Volume 2* by Stephen Fite (Melody House)
"How Much Is That Doggie in the Window?" from *Great Big Hits* by Sharon, Lois, and Bram (Drive)

Sing a Song of Bingo

Materials
none

Use the Dog Stuffed-Animal Puppet to lead children in a round of "Bingo" to give them some extra practice with phoneme substitution. Invite children to change one or more of the letters in the name Bingo to create a new five-letter word, such as *Pingo, Bongo,* or *Binky.* Invite children to sing the song again with one of the names they suggested.

Little Counting Dog

Materials
none

Tell children that you know a little dog that likes to bark. Show the class the Dog Stuffed-Animal Puppet. Ask children to listen carefully to the number of times the dog barks in the verse below. Show the puppet as you chant, but place it behind your back after the fourth line.

> *My little counting dog*
> *Barked one sunny day.*
> **Woof! Woof! Woof!**
> *Then he ran away.*

Ask children to raise the number of fingers that identifies the number of times the dog barked. Change the number of barks in the boldfaced line, and repeat the verse.

Songs

Dinosaur Glove Puppet

Materials
Spikes pattern (page 136)
scissors
rubber glove
felt
stapler
permanent marker

Directions
Cut a slit from the wrist to the middle finger on the side opposite the palm of a rubber glove. Make a copy of the Spikes pattern, and cut it out. Trace the pattern on a piece of felt, cut it out, and staple it to the back of the glove. Use a permanent marker to draw dots along the back and eyes on the middle finger. The other four fingers will be the dinosaur's legs.

•••

Variation
Instead of spikes, attach fur to the back of the glove to create a tail for a squirrel puppet.

Reading Recommendations
A Dinosaur Named After Me by Bernard Most
Dinosaur Romp by Paul Strickland
Dinosaurs Dancing by Luella Connelly (Creative Teaching Press)
If the Dinosaurs Came Back by Bernard Most
The Mysterious Tadpole by Stephen Kellogg

Song Suggestions
"At the Dinosaur Baseball Game" from *Peppermint Wings* by Linda Arnold (Youngheart Music)
"The Dinosaur Bop" from *The Best of Melody House* by Stephen Fite (Melody House)
"If I Had a Dinosaur" from *The Singable Songs Collection* by Raffi (Rounder Records)
"Please Don't Bring a Tyrannosaurus Rex to Show and Tell" from *Late Last Night* by Joe Scruggs (Lyrick Studios)

A Dinosaur Dance

Materials
songs about dinosaurs (see page 68)
CD/cassette player

Play songs about dinosaurs, and have the Dinosaur Glove Puppet lead the class as they stomp around the room like dinosaurs. Use synonyms for the word *big* (e.g., *huge, gigantic, colossal*) to describe children's movements.

Dazzling Dinosaur Designs

Materials
A Dinosaur Named After Me by Bernard Most
rubber gloves
felt
scissors
stapler
art supplies (e.g., stickers, ricrac, fabric scraps, pipe cleaners, sequins, glitter, markers)

Have the Dinosaur Glove Puppet read aloud *A Dinosaur Named After Me*. Discuss with the class how the children's names are incorporated into the names of the dinosaurs (e.g., *Susan-osaurus* or *Miles-osaurus*). Invite an adult volunteer to help children make individual dinosaur puppets. Distribute to each child a rubber glove with a spiky felt back stapled to it. Have children use art supplies to personalize their puppet. Encourage children to add *-osaurus* to their own name to create a name for their puppet.

Animal Paper-Sack Puppets

Materials
animal patterns (pages 137–141)
scissors
construction paper
art supplies (e.g., markers, construction paper)
glue
paper lunch sacks

Directions
Make a copy of an animal pattern, and cut it out. Trace the pattern onto a sheet of construction paper, cut it out, and decorate it with art supplies. Laminate the cutout, and glue it to a paper lunch sack.

●●

Variation
Invite children to draw, color, and cut out a picture of the head of their favorite animal. Laminate each head before gluing it to a paper lunch sack to keep these adorable animal puppets from becoming "endangered."

Reading Recommendations
From Head to Toe by Eric Carle
Mice Squeak, We Speak by Tomie dePaola
Noah's Ark by Lucy Cousins
Noah's Ark by Peter Spier

Song Suggestions
"Alphabet Zoo" from *ABC Chicka Boom with Me* by John Archambault and David Plummer (Creative Teaching Press)
"Animal Quiz Part One" and "Animal Quiz Part Two" from *Can a Cherry Pie Wave Goodbye?* by Hap Palmer (Hap Palmer Recordings)
"Going to the Zoo" from *The Singable Songs Collection* by Raffi (Rounder Records)

From Head to Toe

Materials

From Head to Toe by Eric Carle

In advance, make an Animal Paper-Sack Puppet for each child. Use the animals from the book *From Head to Toe*. Read aloud the story, and ask children to name the animals that appear in it. Give each child a puppet. Reread the story, and encourage children to hold their puppet and perform the actions of their animal when it is named in the story.

Mice Squeak

Materials

Mice Squeak, We Speak by Tomie dePaola

In advance, make an Animal Paper-Sack Puppet for each child. Use the animals from the book *Mice Squeak, We Speak*. Read aloud the story, and ask children to name the animals that appear in it. Give each child a puppet. Reread the story, and encourage children to listen for their animal, imitate its sound, and pantomime its movement with their puppet.

Tiger Kitchen-Mitt Puppet

Materials
scissors
orange, pink, white, and black felt
glue gun
orange kitchen mitt
black pipe cleaners
wiggly eyes

Directions
Cut triangular ears from orange felt, and glue them to the top of the mitt. Cut a nose from pink felt. Place the mitt on your hand, and bend your fingers to create a mouth. Glue the pink felt nose on the mitt. Remove the mitt from your hand, and glue black pipe cleaners beneath the nose for whiskers. Glue on wiggly eyes. Cut small pointed teeth from white felt and a tongue from pink felt, and glue them inside the mouth. Cut stripes from black felt, and glue them along the "body."

Variation
Purchase a kitchen mitt, a hot pad, or a child's bath mitt that features the face of an animal, and use it as a puppet.

Reading Recommendations
Little Tiger Goes to School by Julie Sykes
Tiger Called Thomas by Charlotte Zolotow
We're Going on a Bear Hunt by Michael Rosen and Helen Oxenbury

Song Suggestions
"Tiger with a Toothbrush" from *We're on Our Way* by Hap Palmer (Hap Palmer Recordings)

Going on a Tiger Hunt

Materials

none

Use the Tiger Kitchen-Mitt Puppet to lead the class on an imaginary tiger hunt. Invite children to name places a tiger might go, such as around mud or through a forest. Use children's suggestions to replace the boldfaced words in the following variation of "We're Going on a Bear Hunt." Encourage children to chant along with the puppet and pantomime actions for the words.

We're going on a tiger hunt.
We're going on a tiger hunt.
We're going to catch a big one.
Are you scared? NO!

*There's **a river** ahead.*
Can't go over it.
Can't go under it.
*Have to go **through** it!*
Swim, swim, swim, swim!

*There's **mud** ahead.*
Can't go over it.
Can't go under it.
*Have to go **around** it!*
Squish, squish, squish, squish!

Use a mitt with a different animal or choose a different puppet from this book, and change the word *tiger* in the first verse to reflect the new animal puppet (e.g., bear, elephant, duck). Also, change the names of the places the new animal puppet might go.

Wild Thing Grocery-Sack Mask

Materials

scissors
paper grocery sack
art supplies (e.g., ricrac, bows, ribbons, crepe paper, silk flowers, tissue paper, pipe cleaners, pieces of bright fabric cut in strips, glue)

Directions

Cut out large eye holes in a paper grocery sack. Use art supplies to personalize your mask.

● ●

Variation

Cut out a 6" (15 cm) square from a paper sack. Use markers to draw a frame or the cabinet for a television set around the square. Invite children to wear the mask to pose for a painting or perform a television show.

Reading Recommendations

Glad Monster, Sad Monster by Ed Emberley and Anne Miranda
One Hungry Monster by Susan O'Keefe
Where Do Monsters Live? by Rozanne Lanczak Williams (Creative Teaching Press)
Where the Wild Things Are by Maurice Sendak

Song Suggestions

"Games Monsters Play" from *Monster Melodies* by Sesame Street (Sony Wonder)

The Wild Things Are Here

Materials

Where the Wild Things Are by Maurice Sendak
art supplies (e.g., ricrac, bows, ribbons, crepe paper, silk flowers, tissue paper, pipe cleaners, pieces of bright fabric cut in strips)
CD/cassette tape with any prerecorded music
CD/cassette player

Read aloud *Where the Wild Things Are*. Have each child use art supplies to make a Wild Thing Grocery-Sack Mask. Reread the story, and encourage children to wear their mask. When you read the words *Let the wild rumpus start*, play music, and invite the class to get up and dance. Stop the music, and say *Now stop*, and have children sit down to listen to the end of the story.

All-the-Makings for a Monster

Materials

art supplies (e.g., ricrac, bows, ribbons, crepe paper, silk flowers, tissue paper, pipe cleaners, pieces of bright fabric cut in strips)

Have each child make a Wild Thing Grocery-Sack Mask that has a special name and personality. Tell children to think of something silly their monster likes to do (e.g., eat marshmallows, play hopscotch, sing), and have them decorate their mask to reflect this. Encourage children to act out what their monster likes to do.

Movement

Simon, the Sponge-Paintbrush Puppet

Materials
glue gun
wiggly eyes
sponge paintbrush
art supplies (e.g., ricrac, bows,
    ribbons, crepe paper,
    silk flowers, tissue paper,
    pipe cleaners, pieces
    of bright fabric cut in strips)

Directions
Glue wiggly eyes to a sponge paintbrush. Use art supplies to personalize the puppet.

Variation
Add wings cut from black construction paper to create a bat puppet.

Reading Recommendations
I See Patterns by Linda Benton (Creative Teaching Press)
Mr. Noisy's Book of Patterns by Rozanne Lanczak Williams (Creative Teaching Press)

Song Suggestions
"Simon Says" from *We All Live Together, Volume 3* by Greg & Steve (Youngheart Music)
"Simple Simon" from *Mainly Mother Goose* by Sharon, Lois, and Bram (Drive)

Sponge-Painted Patterns

Materials

sponges cut into various shapes
heavy paper
paint (assorted colors)

Invite children to work with a partner or small group. Give each pair or group sponges that have been cut into various shapes, a piece of heavy paper, and paint. Have Simon explain to children how to use two sponges and two different colors of paint to form a pattern. Have the puppet praise the children as they work by saying things such as *Your pattern is yellow star, yellow star, red circle. Very good!* or *I can tell from your pattern that orange comes after blue.*

What Does Simon Say?

Materials

none

Use Simon in a game of Simon Says. Perform an action, and have Simon give children directions to follow, such as *Simon says, "Tap your foot," Simon says, "Slap your knee,"* or *Simon says, "Touch your cheek."* To test that children are listening carefully, give one direction, but do the opposite. For example, say *Touch your head,* but touch your toe or say *Pat your back,* but rub your tummy.

Snail Stocking Puppet

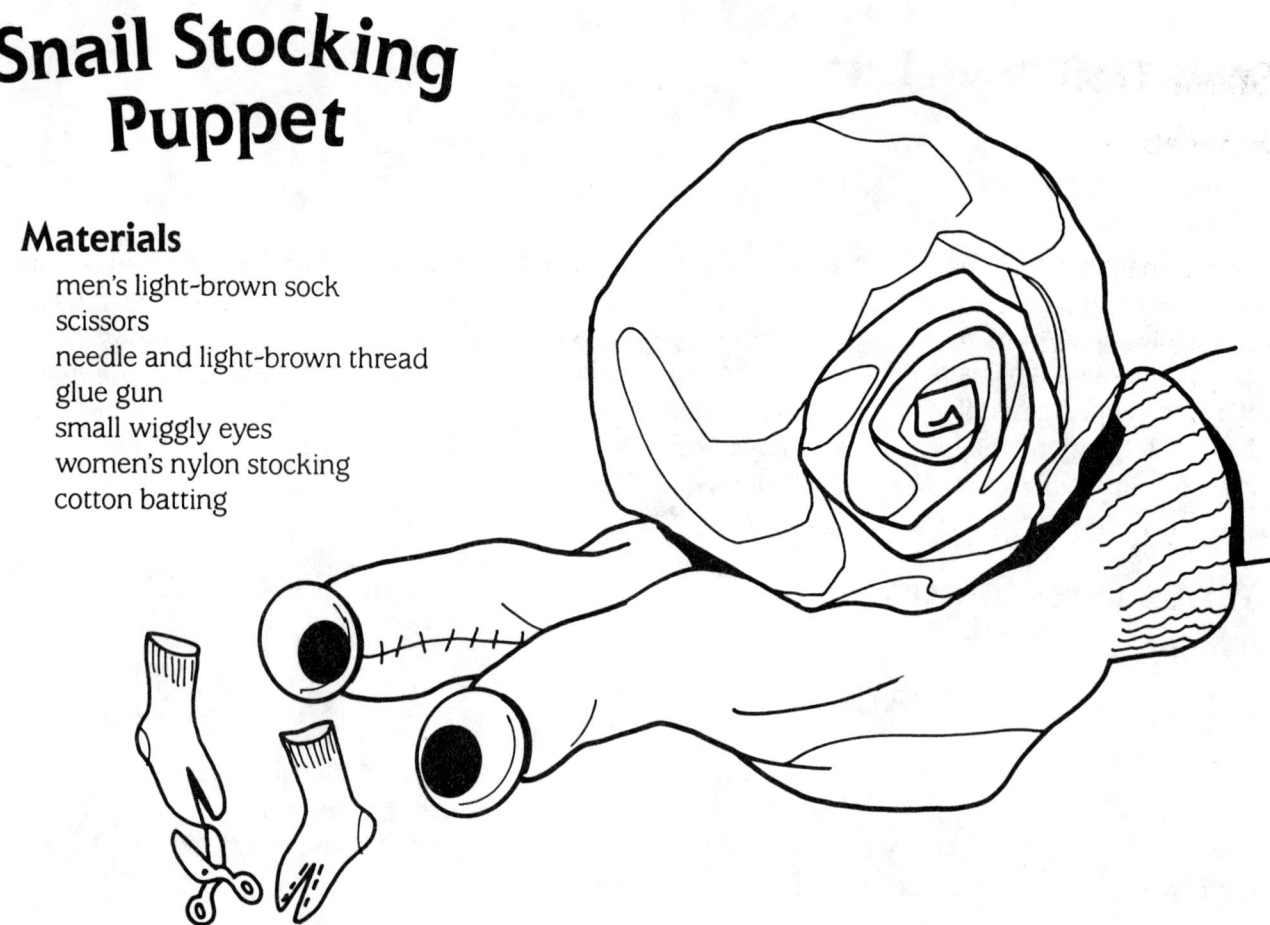

Materials

men's light-brown sock
scissors
needle and light-brown thread
glue gun
small wiggly eyes
women's nylon stocking
cotton batting

Directions

Turn the sock inside out. Make a straight cut approximately 3" (7.5 cm) in from the toe towards the ankle of the sock. Stitch the sides together to create two antennae (as shown). Turn the sock right side out. Glue a wiggly eye to the top of each antenna. Stuff a nylon stocking with cotton batting, and wind it into a coil. Sew the coil in place, and attach it to the top of the sock with glue or a needle and thread.

●●

Variation

Omit the step in which the antennae are cut and sewn. Instead, add legs cut from brown or orange felt to a sand-colored sock to create a hermit crab puppet.

Reading Recommendations

Snail by Chris Henwood
Snail Spell by Joanne Ryder
Snail, Where Are You? by Tomi Ungerer

Song Suggestions

"Copy Cat" from *Kidding Around* by Greg & Steve (Youngheart Music)
"Just Like Me (Mirror Movement)" from *We All Live Together, Volume 4* by Greg & Steve (Youngheart Music)

Snail Trail

Materials

none

Use the Snail Stocking Puppet to lead this version of the game Follow the Leader. Ask one child to hold the puppet and be the leader. Have the rest of the class stand in a group before the leader. Explain that the leader will perform an action for the other children to follow. As children perform the action, use descriptive words to describe their movement. For example, use the words *slowly, slippery, slimy,* and *slide* to describe a child who is pantomiming a snail.

Sound It Out S-L-O-W-L-Y

Materials

none

Use the Snail Stocking Puppet to name words for the class to sound out. Prompt children with the following poem:

> *I'm a snail who likes to rhyme,*
> *And when I read I take my time.*
> *Each new word I happen to see*
> *I sound out very carefully.*
> *Now's the time to try one with me.*
> *Say the sounds of **cat** very slo—wly.*

Prompt children to say /c/ /a/ /t/. Change the boldfaced word, and repeat the activity.

Games

Stoplight Sponge Puppet

Materials
glue gun
red, yellow, and green plastic-mesh scrubber sponges
paint-stirring stick
small wiggly eyes

Directions
Glue three mesh sponges to a paint-stirring stick in the following order: red on top, yellow in the middle, and green on the bottom. Glue a pair of wiggly eyes to each sponge.

Variation
Spray paint three mesh sponges white, and glue them on the paint-stirring stick. Cut out a hat, a nose, arms, and circles from black construction paper, and add them to the sponges to create a snowman puppet.

Reading Recommendations
Go, Dog, Go! by P. D. Eastman
Red Light, Green Light, Mama and Me by Cari Best
Safety Counts! by Joel Kupperstein (Creative Teaching Press)

Song Suggestions
"Body Rock" from *Kidding Around* by Greg & Steve (Youngheart Music)

Stop-and-Go Game

Materials

none

Use the Stoplight Sponge Puppet for a game of Stoplight. Have children line up on one side of the room or a large playing field. Hold the puppet, and stand on the opposite side of the playing area. Explain to the class that when you call *green light* they should run towards the puppet and that when you call *red light* they should stop running. Alternate calling out *green light* and *red light* until each child reaches the puppet.

Stop and Think

Materials

none

Use the Stoplight Sponge Puppet to help children "stop and think" about what they are doing. For example, if you see two children arguing over a toy, hold up the puppet and say *Stop and think!* Then, encourage the children to name ways to solve their problem without arguing. Or, use the puppet to help children think about other ways they act in the classroom. Choose a comment that applies to their particular situation. For example, say *Stop and listen, Stop and make another choice, Stop and give yourself a pat on the back,* or *Stop and do that again . . . that was great!*

Games

Ace, the Racquet Puppet

Materials
glue gun
2 small white cardboard circles
child's tennis or badminton racquet
wiggly eyes
golf balls
tennis ball

Directions
Glue two small white cardboard circles for eyes to a child's tennis or badminton racquet. Glue a wiggly eye to each of two golf balls, and glue the balls to the cardboard circles to complete the eyes. Glue on a tennis ball for the nose.

Variation
Cut a head, tail, and four legs from yellow construction paper. Glue the head to the end of the handle and the legs and tail to the face of the racquet to create a giraffe puppet.

Reading Recommendations
Anna Banana: 101 Jump-Rope Rhymes by Joanna Cole
Let's Play: Traditional Games of Childhood by Camilla Gryski
Shimmy Shimmy Coke-Ca-Pop! by John and Carol Langstaff

Song Suggestions
"Bale of Hay" from *The Corner Grocery Store* by Raffi (Rounder Records)
"Jump Rope Rhymes" from *ABC Chicka Boom with Me* by John Archambault and David Plummer (Creative Teaching Press)
"The Things We Like to Do" from *We're On Our Way* by Hap Palmer (Hap Palmer Recordings)

Who's Making That Racket?

Materials
>none

Explain to children that a *racket* can also be a loud noise. Display Ace and invite children to name things that make a loud noise. Invite the class to make the noise (e.g., *boom boom* for drum, *meow* for cat).

We LOVE This Game

Materials
>none

Arrange children in a circle, and have them say the following rhyme as they pass Ace around the circle:
>*One love, two love, three love, four.*
>*Five love, six love, seven love, MORE!*

Ask children to stop passing the puppet when they hear the word *MORE*. Tell the child who is holding the puppet *You've won! You get to sit down. Now let's go on and see who wins next.* Continue until each child "wins," and the whole class is seated.

Games

83

Silhouette Felt Puppet

Materials

Body pattern (page 128)
scissors
felt
needle and thread (optional)
glue gun
wiggly eyes
yarn
art supplies (e.g., ricrac, bows, ribbons, crepe paper, tissue paper, pipe cleaners, pieces of bright fabric cut in strips)

Directions

Make a copy of the Body pattern, and cut it out. Place together two pieces of felt, and trace the pattern on the top piece. Cut out both shapes, and stitch or glue them together, leaving the bottom edge open. Use glue to attach a pair of wiggly eyes and yarn for hair. Decorate the puppet with art supplies.

•••

Variation

Copy the Body pattern onto white paper and add black eyes and a mouth to create a ghost puppet.

Reading Recommendations

My Many Colored Days by Dr. Seuss
One of Each by Mary Ann Hoberman

Song Suggestions

"Friends" from *On the Move* by Greg & Steve (Youngheart Music)
"You Are My Friend" from *Making Moosic* by Anna Moo (Anna Moo Good Moo's Productions)

Our Many Colored Puppets

Materials

My Many Colored Days by Dr. Seuss

In advance, use the Body pattern to create several Silhouette Felt Puppets in various colors. Read aloud *My Many Colored Days*, and invite a few children to use the puppets to retell the story. Encourage children to use the puppets at other times during the day to show when they are feeling happy, sad, excited, worried, or frustrated.

One of Each

Materials

One of Each by Mary Ann Hoberman
Body pattern (page 128)
scissors
glue
paper
crayons or markers

Read aloud *One of Each*. Give each child two copies of the Body pattern to cut out and glue to a piece of paper. Ask children to think of something that they like to do with a friend. Encourage children to use crayons or markers to decorate the cutouts as themselves and a friend doing something special together. Ask children to write and complete the sentence *With a friend, I can* _____ on their paper. Display children's work around the room.

Exploring Emotions

Peek-a-Boo Stick Puppet

Materials
glue
wiggly eyes
small pom-pom ball
tongue depressor

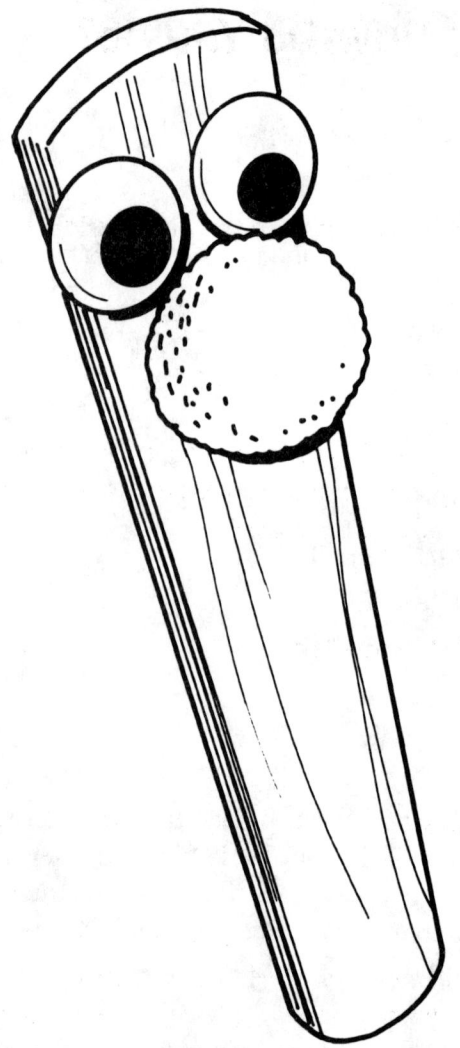

Directions
Glue wiggly eyes and a small pom-pom ball for a nose to a tongue depressor to create a simple Peek-a-Boo Stick Puppet.

•••

Variation
Add brown pipe cleaners for antlers and use a marker to draw a nose and a mouth to create a moose or reindeer puppet.

Reading Recommendations
Alexander and the Terrible, Horrible, No Good Very Bad Day by Judith Viorst
Oh, Were They Ever Happy by Peter Spier
On Monday When It Rained by Cheryl Kachenmeister
The Tenth Good Thing about Barney by Judith Viorst

Song Suggestions
"If You're Happy and You Know It" from *We All Live Together, Volume 3* by Greg & Steve (Youngheart Music)

Peek-a-Boo, How Do You Do?

Materials
none

Hide the Peek-a-Boo Stick Puppet in your pocket. Pull out the puppet, and say
> Peek-a-Boo!
> How do you do?
> I feel **happy**.
> How about you?

Invite children who are feeling happy to raise their hand. Ask for volunteers to explain why they are feeling happy. Change the boldfaced word to a word that describes a different emotion (e.g., *silly, sad, mad, worried*), and repeat the activity.

Yes, No, Maybe So

Materials
tongue depressors
wiggly eyes
small pom-pom balls
glue
red markers

Invite children to make their own Peek-a-Boo Stick Puppet to use during class discussions. Give each child a tongue depressor, two pairs of wiggly eyes, and two small pom-pom balls. Show children how to glue a pair of eyes and a pom-pom ball nose to each side of their tongue depressor. Have children use a red marker to draw a smile on one side of the stick and a frown on the other side. Ask children to use their puppet to answer *yes* or *no* during group discussions. For example, during a lesson about animals on a farm, ask the class questions such as *Do goats live on a farm? Is a baby horse called a calf?* and *Does wool come from sheep?* Encourage children to answer each question by showing the happy side of their puppet for *yes* and the sad side of their puppet for *no*.

Exploring Emotions

Anyone Felt Puppet

Materials
Body pattern (page 128)
scissors
felt
needle and thread (optional)
glue gun
plastic craft head or a large wooden bead
art supplies (e.g., wiggly eyes, yarn, ricrac, bows, ribbons, crepe paper, tissue paper, pipe cleaners, scraps of bright fabric)

Directions
Make a copy of the Body pattern, and cut it out. Place together two pieces of felt, and trace the pattern on the top piece. Cut out both shapes, and stitch or glue them together, leaving the bottom edge open. Glue a plastic craft head or large wooden bead to the body. Use art supplies to personalize the puppet.

Variation
Use art supplies to dress the Anyone Felt Puppet for a career as an astronaut, a diver, a train engineer, or a zookeeper.

Reading Recommendations
Little Beaver and the Echo by Amy MacDonald
Shy Charles by Rosemary Wells
Today I Feel Silly and Other Moods That Make My Day by Jamie Lee Curtis

Song Suggestions
"Magical, Miracle, Me" from *I'm a Can-Do Kid* by John Archambault and David Plummer (Creative Teaching Press)

Again, with Feeling

Materials
> none

Use the Anyone Felt Puppet to tell a story that relates to a problem that has occurred in the classroom. For example, have the puppet tell children *I am Andrew. I feel sad when my mommy leaves me at school each day. I miss my mommy, so I cry.* Encourage children to offer solutions to the puppet's problem. Other stories might be about biting, sharing, wearing glasses, using a wheelchair, or forgetting to bring lunch to school.

A Character Actor

Materials
> art supplies (e.g., ricrac, bows, ribbons, crepe paper, tissue paper, sequins, yarn, fabric scraps, pipe cleaners, construction paper)
> scissors
> glue gun

Use the Anyone Felt Puppet to bring to life children's favorite characters from familiar songs, poems, and stories. For example, personalize the puppet to represent the old lady who swallowed a fly, Peter Pumpkin-Eater, or Goldilocks. Use art supplies to add features that are particular to each character. For example, attach pipe-cleaner glasses for the old lady, a construction paper pumpkin for Peter, and a mop of yellow yarn hair for Goldilocks. Encourage children to use the puppets to retell the stories during a free-choice period.

Exploring Emotions

High-Five Flyswatter Puppet

Materials
scissors
yarn
glue gun
flyswatter
construction paper

Directions
Cut several 12" (30.5 cm) pieces of yarn, and separate them into two bundles. Braid each bundle, and glue the braids on a flyswatter. Glue some short, loose pieces of yarn to the top of the flyswatter to create bangs. Cut out eyes, a nose, and a mouth from construction paper, and glue them onto the flyswatter to form a face.

Variation
Add petals and leaves cut from colored construction paper to create a flower puppet.

Reading Recommendations
I Am Special by Kimberly Jordano (Creative Teaching Press)
I Can Do It Myself by Lessee Little and Eloise Greenfield
I Like Me by Nancy Carlson
The One and Only Special Me by Rozanne Lanczak Williams (Creative Teaching Press)

Song Suggestions
"Flick a Fly" from *Walter the Waltzing Worm* by Hap Palmer (Educational Activities, Inc.)
"I'm So Proud of You" from *Making Moosic* by Anna Moo (Anna Moo Good Moo's Productions)

Give Me Five!

Materials
　none

When children have completed a task or finished a project, use the High-Five Flyswatter Puppet to gently tap their hand to give them a high five.

Swat That Word!

Materials
　marker
　sentence strips or index cards

Use a marker to write sight words or vocabulary words on sentence strips or index cards, and display them on a board or wall. Invite individual children to hold the High-Five Flyswatter Puppet and stand beside the board or wall. Say a word, and ask the child to use the puppet to gently "swat" the word on the wall that matches it.

Butterfly Finger Puppet

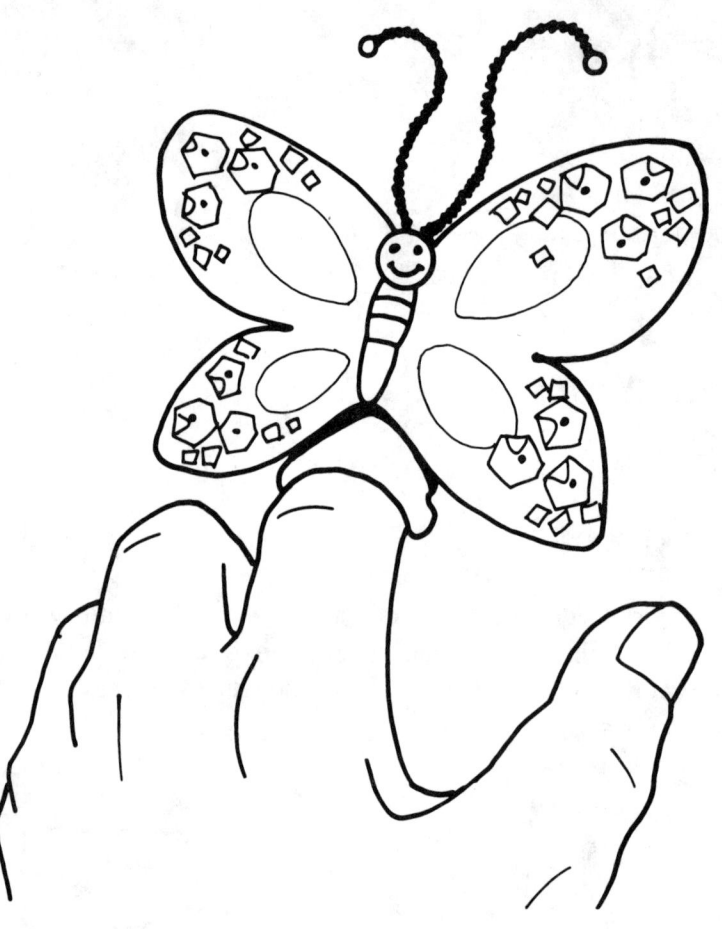

Materials
Butterfly pattern (page 142)
scissors
felt
glue gun
sequins
men's cotton work glove

Directions
Make a copy of the Butterfly pattern, and cut it out. Trace the pattern on a piece of felt, and cut it out. Glue sequins on the wings. Cut a finger from the glove, and glue it to the back of the butterfly. Place the puppet over your finger, and move it so the wings appear to flutter.

Variation
Cut out a pair of airplane wings and a propeller from tagboard. Glue the wings to the back side of the glove finger, and use a metal fastener to attach the propeller to the tip of the finger. Use a marker to draw windows for this airplane finger puppet.

Reading Recommendations
An Invitation to the Butterfly Ball by Jane Yolen
When I Get Bigger by Mercer Mayer
Where Butterflies Grow by Joanne Ryder
Where Does the Butterfly Go When It Rains? by May Garelick

Song Suggestions
"Butterfly" from *Peppermint Wings* by Linda Arnold (Youngheart Music)
"I Wonder If I'm Growing" from *The Singable Songs Collection* by Raffi (Rounder Records)
"I'm a Can-Do Kid" from *I'm a Can-Do Kid* by John Archambault and David Plummer (Creative Teaching Press)

Until Butter Flies

Materials
- drawing paper
- crayons or markers
- bookbinding materials

Use the Butterfly Finger Puppet to introduce compound words. Ask children to name the two words that combine to make the word *butterfly*. Encourage children to imagine a stick of butter that is flying. Ask children to name other words that are made of two smaller words, such as *dragonfly, eggroll,* and *homework*. Invite children to draw a silly picture that represents the two small words that make one compound word. Bind the children's work together into a book titled *Until Butter Flies,* and place it in your reading center or class library.

Butterfly Kisses

Materials
- none

Use the Butterfly Finger Puppet to give children soft "butterfly kisses" as a reward for doing a good job or to awaken children after nap time.

Drizzle, the Watering-Can Puppet

Materials
glue gun
large wiggly eyes
child's plastic watering can
3" (7.5 cm) square scarf
or piece of fabric

Directions
Glue large wiggly eyes to the front of a child's plastic watering can. Wrap a scarf or piece of fabric around your hand to hide it, and then place it inside the watering can. (If your hand does not fit inside the can, grasp the handle.)

• •

Variation
Do not invert the can. Place the wiggly eyes above the spout (the nose), and use this puppet to hold rulers or bookmarks for the class.

Reading Recommendations
I am a Seed by Jean Marzollo
I am Water by Jean Marzollo
See How It Grows by Kimberlee Graves (Creative Teaching Press)
Your First Garden Book by Marc Brown

Song Suggestions
"Grow & Grow & Grow" from *Anna Banana* by Kathleen Gibson (Rompin' Records)

A Shower of Praise

Materials

none

Invite children to name things plants need to grow. Ask children to identify things they need to help their bodies grow, such as food, water, and sleep. Explain to children that there are other things that we cannot see or touch that help us "grow" as people. Tell children that when we feel good about ourselves, we grow healthy and happy. Choose a child to sit before the class. Use Drizzle to "sprinkle" a compliment over this child's head. For example, tip the puppet over the child's head and say *Madeline remembered to say please and thank you.* Invite other children to use the puppet to compliment a classmate. Repeat the activity with another child until each member of the class has received a "shower" of praise!

How Does Your Garden Grow?

Materials

water
cotton ball
radish seed or lima bean
resealable plastic bag
tape

Use Drizzle to introduce a lesson on how plants grow. The fast-growing garden used in this activity is easy for children to view. Place a wet cotton ball and a radish seed or lima bean inside a resealable plastic bag. Seal the bag, tape it to a window, and invite children to use Drizzle to "water" it each day. When the seed or bean sprouts, encourage children to discuss the changes they observe. Have the puppet praise children for their contributions to the discussion.

Mop-Head Puppet

Materials
tongue depressor
2" (5 cm) Styrofoam ball
glue gun
puff paint
scissors
⅔ yard (61 cm) bright cotton fabric
red yarn

Directions
Insert a tongue depressor into a Styrofoam ball, and glue it in place. Use puff paint to add facial features to the ball. Cut a circle with a 12" (30.5 cm) diameter from fabric. Cut a small hole in the center of the fabric, and insert the tongue depressor. Glue the fabric to the ball. Cut several strands of red yarn, and glue them to the top of the ball.

●●●

Variation
Use yellow yarn and denim fabric and add straw to the collar to create a scarecrow puppet.

Reading Recommendations
I Was So Mad by Mercer Mayer
Lily and the Purple, Plastic Purse by Kevin Henkes
Playground Problem Solvers by Sandi Hill (Creative Teaching Press)
There's a Hole in the Bucket by Nadine Bernard Westcott

Song Suggestions
"The Fox and the Chicken" from *I'm a Can-Do Kid* by John Archambault and David Plummer (Creative Teaching Press)

A Pair of Problem Solvers

Materials

none

Make two Mop-Head Puppets, and give them names, such as Abigale and Albert. Use the puppets to help children solve problems. Ask the puppets questions that relate to a problem a child or children in class are having. For example, after a situation in which hitting was involved, use puppets to discuss what happened. Use the following dialogue as an example:

Teacher: *What happened Albert?*
Albert: *Abigale hit me.*
Teacher: *Abigale, why did you hit Albert?*
Abigale: *He was bothering me.*
Teacher: *Is it OK to hit others, Abigale?*
Abigale: *No, but I was mad.*
Teacher: *Class, what could Abigale do when she gets mad at Albert instead of hit him?*

Use the puppets when other problems arise, or make them available to children to practice problem-solving techniques throughout the day.

In the First Place

Materials

none

Invite two or three children to stand in a line before the class. Ask the first child in line to hold the Mop-Head Puppet. Say *Mop Head is **first** in line. Who is **last**?* Invite children to name the child who is standing last in line. Change the boldfaced words to reflect other ordinal words (e.g., *Mop Head is **third** in line. Who is **second**?*). Invite new children to stand in a line before the class, and repeat the activity.

Fuzzy Wuzzy Cuddlebug Slipper Puppet

Materials
fuzzy slipper
glue gun
wiggly eyes
scissors
felt (assorted colors)

Directions
Bend the slipper in half. Glue on a pair of wiggly eyes at the toe of the slipper. Cut lips, teeth, eyebrows, and other facial features from felt, and glue them onto the puppet. To manipulate the puppet, insert your hand into the opening and bend the slipper in half.

Variation
Use art supplies to transform a fuzzy slipper into a bear, a raccoon, or another furry animal to make a cute and cuddly puppet.

Reading Recommendations
The Kissing Hand by Audrey Penn
Love You Forever by Robert Munsch
Love You the Purplest by Barbara M. Joosse
Will You Take Care of Me? by Margaret Park Bridges

Song Suggestions
"Hugging Song" and "Love Is" from *Holidays and Special Times* by Greg & Steve (Youngheart Music)
"Love Changes Everything" from *Making Moosic* by Anna Moo (Anna Moo Good Moo's Productions)

A Hug for a Cuddlebug

Materials

none

Use Fuzzy Wuzzy Cuddlebug to help you recite the following couplets. Encourage children to answer each question the puppet asks.

Fuzzy Wuzzy Cuddlebug is looking for a hug.
Is there anybody here to hug a cuddlebug?

Poor Fuzzy Wuzzy—his mom and dad he misses.
Is there anybody here who can help him with some kisses?

When Fuzzy Wuzzy is afraid he sheds a little tear.
Will someone whisper "It's OK" into his little ear?

Someone told Fuzzy Wuzzy, "You're not my friend today."
Does anybody know how to take this hurt away?

Oh, Fuzzy Wuzzy, he's so mad, 'cause someone took his ball.
Can we help him problem-solve so he won't be mad after all?

This Puppet's a Picky Eater

Materials

sentence strips or index cards

Explain to children that Fuzzy Wuzzy Cuddlebug has a problem—he only eats words that start with /p/. Ask children to name words that the puppet is able to eat (e.g., *pencil, peanut, paper*), and write them on sentence strips or index cards. To extend learning, change the sound and its placement in the word, and repeat the activity until the puppet is "full"!

Happy/Sad Sylvester Stick Puppet

Materials
scissors
yarn
small index card
glue gun
3" (7.5 cm) Styrofoam ball
wiggly eyes
pom-pom balls
marker
small dowel or chopstick
pinking shears
fabric
½" (13 mm) strip of felt

Directions
Use yarn and an index card to make a pom-pom ball according to the directions on page 28. Glue the yarn pom-pom ball so that it covers the top of a Styrofoam ball. Glue a pair of wiggly eyes and a pom-pom ball to both sides of the Styrofoam ball. Use a marker to draw a smile on one side of the head and a frown on the other side. Insert a dowel or chopstick into the Styrofoam ball. Use pinking shears to cut out a 12" (30.5 cm) circle of fabric. Cut a small hole in the center of the fabric, insert the dowel or chopstick, and glue the fabric under the ball. Glue a thin strip of felt to the bottom of the dowel or chopstick to protect children from harming themselves with the pointed edge. Turn the puppet to change the face from happy to sad.

●●●

Variation
Make one side of the face blue and the other orange before adding features such as chili peppers and icicles to make a Mr. Hot and Mr. Cold Puppet.

Reading Recommendations
If I Were in Charge of the World and Other Worries: Poems for Children and Their Parents by Judith Viorst
Rumpelstiltskin by Paul Galdone
Sad Sam, Blue Sue by Margaret Allen (Creative Teaching Press)
Tough Borris by Mem Fox

Song Suggestions
"Try, Try Again" from *Circus Magic: Under the Big Top* by Linda Arnold (Youngheart Music)

It's All in the Name

Materials

   none

Use Sylvester to tell the class the story of Rumpelstiltskin. Ask children to describe the emotions of the miller's daughter when she could not guess Rumpelstiltskin's name and the feelings of Rumpelstiltskin when the miller's daughter finally did guess his name. Think of a new name (e.g., Frizzle) for the puppet. Invite children to solve a riddle like the following to guess the puppet's name:

   Tell me, can you guess my name?
   Drizzle *and* ***sizzle*** *sound the same.*

After a child guesses the word *Frizzle*, choose a new name for the puppet, change the boldfaced words to words that rhyme with the new name, and repeat the activity.

When You're Happy and You Know It

Materials

   none

Show the class Sylvester's happy face, and ask *How do you think Sylvester feels today? Why do you think he is **happy**? What makes you **happy**?* Encourage children to share their feelings by answering the questions. Turn the puppet around to the sad face, change the boldfaced words to *sad*, and continue the discussion.

Problem Solving

Mr. Peekers Stick Puppet

Materials
Nose pattern (page 143)
wooden dowel or chopstick
2" (5 cm) Styrofoam ball
glue gun
wooden bead
men's brightly colored athletic or soccer sock
scissors
colorful cotton fabric
cotton batting
straight pin
wiggly eyes
pom-pom balls

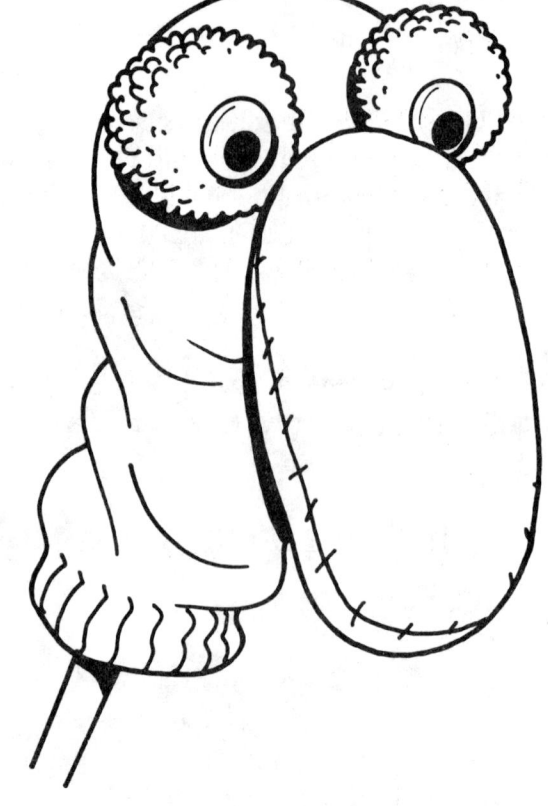

Directions
Insert a wooden dowel or chopstick into a Styrofoam ball, and glue a wooden bead to the other end. Insert the ball into the sock. Make a copy of the Nose pattern, and cut out the pieces. Trace the Nose pattern on a piece of colorful cotton fabric, and cut out both pieces. Glue all but one small edge of the fabric together, and stuff it with cotton batting. Glue the remaining edge of the nose together, attach it to the sock with a straight pin, and glue it in place. Glue wiggly eyes to pom-pom balls, and glue the pom-pom balls to the sock. To move the puppet, hold the dowel or chopstick in one hand and twist it as you slide the sock up and down.

●●

Variation
Use yellow fabric to make the nose and glue brightly colored feathers down the back of the sock to create a toucan puppet.

Reading Recommendations
Clifford's Riddles by Norman Bridwell
Little Critter's Joke Book by Mercer Mayer
My First Riddles by Judith Hoffman Corwin
What Comes in Threes? by Marlene Beierle and Anne Sylvan (Creative Teaching Press)
What Do You See? by Rozanne Lanczak Williams (Creative Teaching Press)

Song Suggestions
"Winding Down" from *Quiet Moments* by Greg & Steve (Youngheart Music)

A Puzzle for Mr. Peekers

Materials
> none

Tell the class that they must guess the correct mystery word in order to make Mr. Peekers pop out. Give some clues about a word, such as *This word is a fruit that is red and starts with a /s/ sound.* Manipulate the puppet so that his head pops up when a child says *strawberry*. Repeat the activity with clues for another word, or try using a number, shape, or color. For example, say *This is the number of feet I have, This is the shape of the clock,* or *This is the color of the sun and a bumblebee.*

Peeking for Parents

Materials
> none

Use Mr. Peekers at the end of the day to notify children when their parents have arrived. Have the puppet "dismiss" each child by saying *Jackie, your mom is here. You may go now* or *Adrian, your dad is here. You may go now.*

Transition Tools

Paddy, the Paddleball Puppet

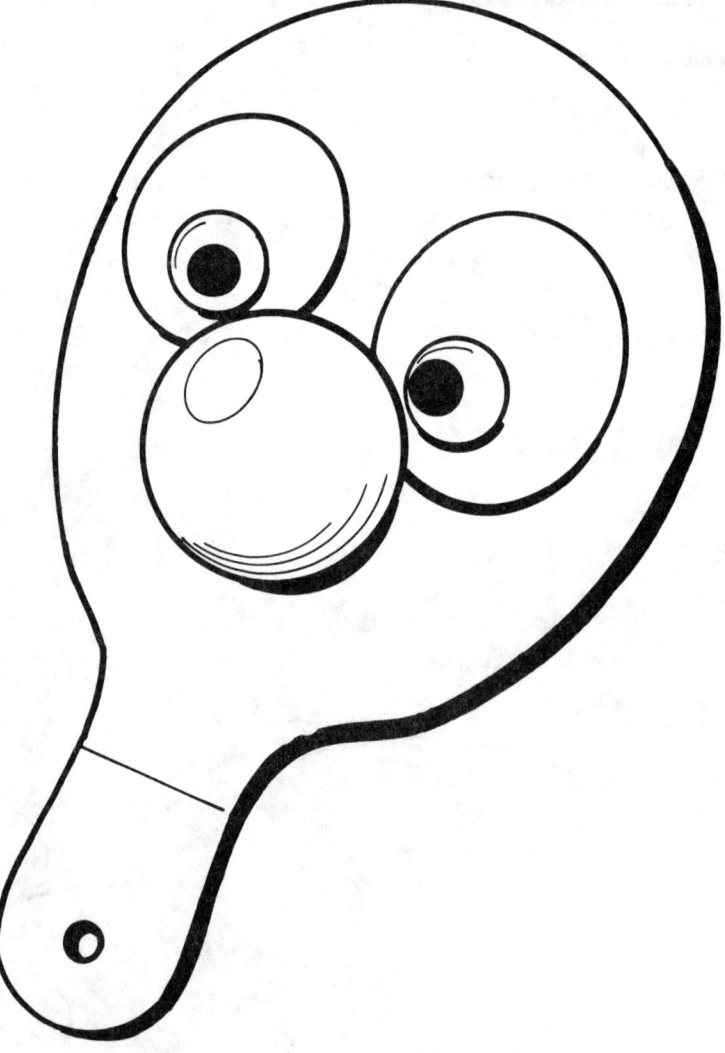

Materials
paddle with rubber ball attached
scissors
white felt
glue gun
large wiggly eyes

Directions
Remove the string that attaches a rubber ball to a paddle. Cut two circles from white felt, and glue them to the paddle for eyes. Glue a wiggly eye to each circle, and glue on the rubber ball for a nose.

•••

Variation
Wrap yarn around plastic curlers and glue them to the top of the paddle. Glue on wiggly eyes, a rubber band for a mouth, and Styrofoam packing pieces for ears to create a Beauty-Shop Bess Puppet.

Reading Recommendations
Mr. Brown Can Moo, Can You? by Dr. Seuss
Polar Bear, Polar Bear, What Do You Hear? by Bill Martin Jr. and Eric Carle

Song Suggestions
"Hip to Hop" from *Nora's Room* by Jessica Harper (Alcazar)

Transition Time

Materials

none

Use Paddy to announce transitions. For example, walk around the room with the puppet, and say *In five minutes it will be time to pick up the toys* or *Follow me to the rug for a story.*

Pass the Paddle

Materials

Mr. Brown Can Moo, Can You? by Dr. Seuss

Read aloud *Mr. Brown Can Moo, Can You?* Invite children to imitate some of the sounds Mr. Brown makes in the story. Arrange children in a circle, and invite a child or two to stand in the middle. Ask these children to make a sound (e.g., *choo-choo, moo, rat-a-tat-tat*) while the rest of the class passes Paddy around the circle. Teach the class the following rhyme to chant as they pass the puppet:

> Let's pass the puppet 'round and 'round
> To **Mike and Cherri's train** sound.

Choose a new child or children to stand in the middle of the circle, and ask them to make a different sound. Change the boldfaced words to reflect the names of the new children and the name of the new sound, and repeat the activity.

Transition Tools

Wibble Wobble Bathroom-Brush Puppet

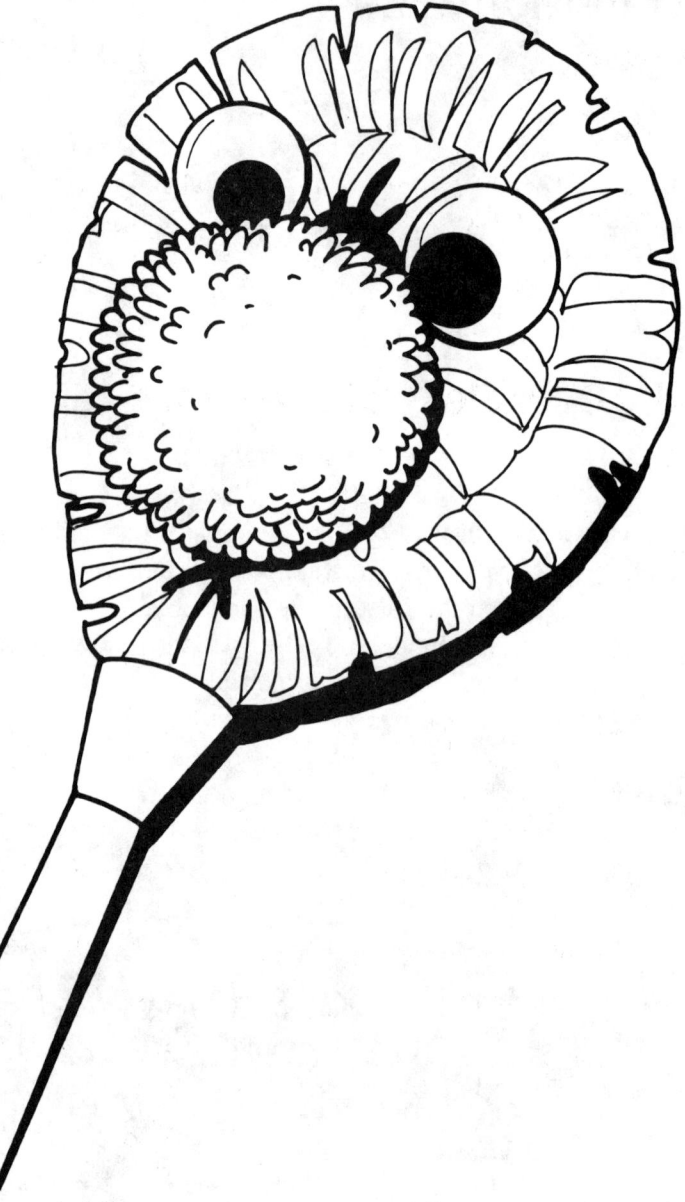

Materials
glue gun
wiggly eyes
large pom-pom ball
bathroom bristle brush with a long handle

Directions
Glue wiggly eyes and a large pom-pom ball for a nose to a bristle brush.

• •

Variation
Dip the brush in brown paint, and let it dry. Add a circular face cut from tagboard to the brush to create a lion puppet.

Reading Recommendations
Sit Still by Nancy Carlson

Song Suggestions
"Wiggle Wobble" from *We All Live Together, Volume 1* by Greg & Steve (Youngheart Music)

Wibble, Wobble—Whoa!

Materials

none

Use Wibble Wobble to signal the end of an activity. Tell children that when they hear *Wibble, wobble—whoa!* they should stop what they are doing and clean up if necessary. For example, wiggle the puppet in the air and call out *Wibble, wobble—whoa!* to end a silent reading period or to indicate that it is time to stop playing a musical instrument.

The Wibble Wobble Seat

Materials

none

Tell the class that Wibble Wobble is looking for quiet children to send outside for recess. Explain to children that when they receive a tap on the shoulder from the puppet they may go outside. Chant the following verses, and use the puppet to dismiss individual children:

Wibble wobble, wibble wobble,
To and fro.
Wibble wobble, wibble wobble,
You can go!

Wibble wobble, wibble wobble,
Pat, pat, pat.
Wibble wobble, wibble wobble,
Scat, scat, scat.

Transition Tools

Mr. Redhead Yarn Puppet

Materials
scissors
red yarn
small index card
glue gun
sewing cone
felt (assorted colors)

Directions
Use yarn and an index card to make a pom-pom ball according to the directions on page 28. Glue the yarn to the top of a sewing cone. Cut ears, eyes, a nose, and a mouth from felt, and glue them onto the cone.

Variation
Paint the cone orange and glue green yarn to the top to create a carrot puppet.

Reading Recommendations
Come along, Daisy by Jane Simmons
Mop Top by Don Freeman
Naptime, Laptime by Eileen Spinelli

Song Suggestions
"Goodbye" from *We All Live Together, Volume 1* by Greg & Steve (Youngheart Music)

Look Ahead, Mr. Redhead

Materials
none

Use Mr. Redhead when it is time for the class to line up. Raise the puppet, and tell children to follow where he leads. Children will happily follow this little guy to lunch, to recess, or during a field trip.

Mr. Redhead's Naptime Rap

Materials
none

Have Mr. Redhead invite children to pantomime the actions in the following verse:
>   *Touch your toes.*
>   *Touch your head.*
>   *Touch your nose.*
>   *Now go to bed.*

Hold the puppet as you walk around the room to supervise children as they settle down for rest time.

Transition Tools

Rooster Stick Puppet

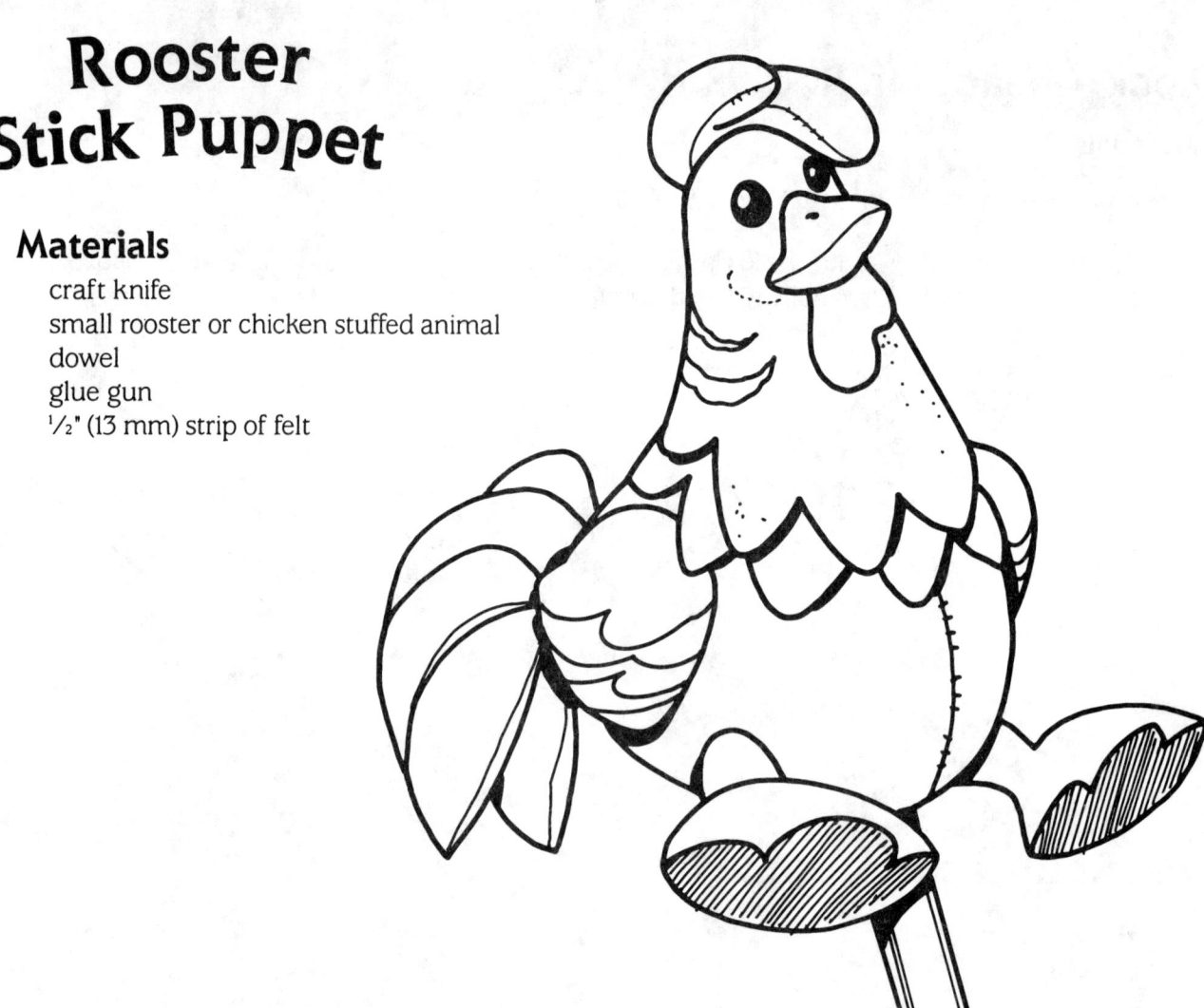

Materials
craft knife
small rooster or chicken stuffed animal
dowel
glue gun
½" (13 mm) strip of felt

Directions
Use a craft knife to cut a small slit in the bottom of a rooster or chicken stuffed animal. Insert a dowel into the slit, and glue the slit shut. Glue a thin strip of felt to the bottom of the dowel to protect children from harming themselves with the pointed edge.

Variation
Substitute any stuffed animal to create this cuddly stick puppet.

Reading Recommendations
Little Red Hen by Paul Galdone
Rooster's Off to See the World by Eric Carle
Rosie's Walk by Pat Hutchins

Song Suggestions
"Cluck, Cluck, Red Hen" by Raffi from *The Singable Songs Collection* (Rounder Records)
"I Had a Rooster" from *Jeremiah Was a Bullfrog!* by Hoyt Axton (Youngheart Music)
"If I Had a Little Rooster" from *The Cat Came Back* by Fred Penner (Youngheart Music)
"Mama's Kitchen" from *Nora's Room* by Jessica Harper (Alcazar)

Cluck, Cluck, It's Time to Get Up

Materials

cassette recorder and cassette (optional)

When it is time for children to get up after rest time, carry the Rooster Stick Puppet around the room and say *Cluck, cluck. It's time to get up!* Or, record a hearty "Cock-a-doodle-doo" on a cassette, and play it as the puppet rouses your slumbering children.

Rosie's Sleep Walk

Materials

Rosie's Walk by Pat Hutchins

Read aloud *Rosie's Walk*. Ask children to describe dangerous situations on the farm that Rosie avoided but the fox did not. Invite children to pretend that they are chicks, and invite them to follow the Rooster Stick Puppet on a walk around the room. Lead children *through* a doorway, *under* a table, *around* a chair, and *down* to their mats for rest time.

Miss Whisper Sleeve Puppet

Materials
scissors
men's long-sleeved shirt
needle and thread
iron-on tape
iron
yarn
ribbon

Directions
Cut a sleeve from the shirt at the shoulder. Turn the sleeve inside out, and sew it shut at the part where it was cut. Turn the sleeve right side out. Arrange iron-on tape at the sewn end of the sleeve to create a face. Use an iron to press the iron-on tape into place. Glue yarn hair to the top of the sleeve. Tie ribbon into a bow, and glue it onto the hair.

Variation
Use a gray shirt and add teeth cut from construction paper to create a shark puppet.

Reading Recommendations
10 Minutes till Bedtime by Peggy Rathman
Goodnight, Gorilla by Peggy Rathman
Good Night, Moon by Margaret Wise Brown
Time to Sleep by Denise Fleming

Song Suggestions
"Body Relaxation" from *Quiet Moments* by Greg & Steve (Youngheart Music)

Whisper Where It Is

Materials
none

Use Miss Whisper to lead a game of Telephone before rest time. Arrange children in a circle. Have the puppet whisper a message (e.g., *We will read a story after rest time* or *We will eat our snack when we get up*) into a child's ear. Invite the child to whisper the message into the ear of the child sitting beside him or her. Encourage children to continue the process until each child has heard the message. Have the last child to receive the message tell it again to the puppet. Have the puppet comment on how the message changed as it traveled around the circle.

With a Whisper

Materials
none

Use Miss Whisper at rest time to whisper in children's ears. Have the puppet tell children what good resters they are. Or, use the puppet to whisper silly secrets, such as *Miss Whisper wishes she had a red ribbon like yours,* or encouraging endearments, such as *Miss Whisper loves caring kids like you.*

Rock-a-Bye Baby Puppet

Materials

old baby doll with cloth body
    and plastic head, hands, and feet
scissors
½ yard (46 cm) fabric
needle and thread
glue gun
lace
ribbon
cotton

Directions

Remove the head and arms from an old baby doll. Cut a 20" x 9" (51 cm x 23 cm) piece of fabric, and fold it in half lengthwise. Stitch or glue the sides of the fabric together, leaving the bottom open and a small space at the top of each side. Cut an opening for the head on the folded side, and leave the bottom open. Glue the head in place, and glue lace around the neckline. Glue an arm to each side of the fabric at the samll space at the top of each side. Tie ribbon into a bow, and stitch it beneath the lace. Put enough cotton in the head to leave space for your finger.

Variation

Design clothes for the baby puppet to wear during different times of the day and seasons.

Reading Recommendations

Barnyard Lullaby by Frank Asch
I Love You, Little One by Nancy Tafuri
More More More, Said the Baby by Vera B. Williams
The Napping House by Audrey Wood
Spot Goes to the Farm by Eric Hill

Song Suggestions

"Down on Grandpa's Farm" and "Hush Little Baby" from *Great Big Hits* by Sharon, Lois, and Bram (Drive)

Sleeping like a Baby

Materials
none

Use the Rock-a-Bye Baby Puppet at rest time. Walk around the room, and tell children that when they are resting quietly the puppet will give them a rest-time hug. Or, use the puppet to help children relax their bodies. Ask children *Are your feet resting? Are your legs resting? Is your head resting?* Praise children by having the puppet say *I like the way you are resting quietly.*

Animal Babies

Materials
Barnyard Lullaby by Frank Asch

Read aloud *Barnyard Lullaby.* Use the Rock-a-Bye Baby Puppet to ask children to recall the different names (e.g., *calf, foal, duckling*) the animals used when they sang their lullabies to their babies in the story. Encourage children to think of the names for other baby animals.

Rest Time

Buster Brush Puppet

Materials
glue gun
bathroom sponge brush
plastic ball
wiggly eyes
marker
yarn

Directions
Glue onto a bathroom sponge brush a plastic ball for a nose and wiggly eyes. Use a marker to draw freckles beside the nose, and glue yarn hair to the top of the "head."

Variation
Omit the yarn hair and add four wheels cut from craft foam to create a racing car puppet.

Reading Recommendations
I Don't Want to Go to Bed by Julie Sykes
Sleepy Bear by Lydia Dabcovich
Wynken, Blynken, & Nod by Eugene Field

Song Suggestions
"Resting" from *We All Live Together, Volume 2* by Greg & Steve (Youngheart Music)

1, 2, 3, What Do You See?

Materials

none

Put Buster Brush to your nose, and recite the following poem:
Buster Brush,
Are you looking at us?
Whom do you see
Resting quietly?

Name all children who are resting quietly. Repeat the poem, and name other children who are now settled for rest time. Change the boldfaced words to reflect other activities the puppet might observe (e.g., *Sharing nicely* or *Coloring neatly*).

Only If…

Materials

none

Use Buster Brush to direct children outside or back to their seats after rest time or story time. Name an item of clothing, a birthday month, or the beginning sound of a first name to dismiss children from the group activity. For example, say *If you are wearing a skirt, you may go outside*, *If you were born in August, you may go back to your seat*, or *If your name starts with an /r/, you may go out and play*.

Rest Time

Mr. Crackers Paintbrush Puppet

Materials
glue gun
3 round wooden drawer pull-handles
wallpaper brush or large paintbrush
wiggly eyes
scissors
felt

Directions
Glue three wooden drawer pull-handles onto one side of a wallpaper brush or large paintbrush to create two eyes and a nose. Glue a wiggly eye to two of the handles. Cut out a felt mouth, and glue it beneath the nose.

Variation
Add sunglasses and some hip clothing to create a rock-star puppet.

Reading Recommendations
Mr. Noisy's Helpers by Rozanne Lanczak Williams (Creative Teaching Press)
Richard Scarry's Busy Workers by Richard Scarry
What Do People Do? by Sarah Willson

Song Suggestions
"Everyone Can Be a Helper" from *Can a Cherry Pie Wave Goodbye?* by Hap Palmer (Hap Palmer Recordings)
"I'd Like to Be an Astronaut" from *I'm a Can-Do Kid* by John Archambault and David Plummer (Creative Teaching Press)

Get Crackin' Mr. Crackers

Materials

none

Have children use Mr. Crackers to help clean off the snack table after they have eaten. Or, invite a child to hold the puppet as the class sings a clean up song.

Mr. Cracker's Assistants

Materials

none

Have Mr. Crackers announce what children should do to help clean up the classroom. For example, have the puppet announce *Katie and David, please clean up the snack table* or *Janet and Ernie, please organize the art supplies.*

Cleanup

Pig Sponge Puppet

Materials
scissors
pink cellulose sponge
glue gun
wiggly eyes
tongue depressor

Directions
Cut out an oval shape from a pink cellulose sponge. Cut two small triangles for ears and a small circle for the nose from leftover sponge pieces. Glue the ears, the nose, and wiggly eyes to the sponge to create a face. Cut a small slit in the bottom of the sponge, and insert a tongue depressor for a handle.

Variation
Cut out shapes such as a blue whale, yellow starfish, or green turtle from sponges to create seashore puppets.

Reading Recommendations
Pigs by Robert Munsch
Pigs by Rozanne Lanczak Williams (Creative Teaching Press)
Pigs Aplenty, Pigs Galore by David McPhail
Those Can-Do Pigs by David McPhail
The Three Little Pigs by Paul Galdone

Song Suggestions
"The Old Sow" from *One Elephant Went out to Play* by Sharon, Lois, and Bram (A&M Records)
"The Sow Took the Measles" from *Little White Duck* by Burl Ives (Columbia Records)

Three Little Pig Puppets

Materials

none

Play this version of This Little Piggy Went to Market to add some fun to a cleanup session. When it is time to clean up the classroom at the end of the day, invite children to stand in a line. Point to the first child in line, and have the Pig Sponge Puppet give him or her a direction such as *This little piggy cleaned the book nook*. Then, point to the next child in line and give him or her a task, too. For example, say *This little piggy picked up blocks* or *This little piggy washed the snack table*. When each child has completed his or her task, direct children to gather their coats and school bags, and dismiss them by saying *And they ran wee, wee, wee, wee all the way home!*

Picking up the Pigpen

Materials

none

Bring out the Pig Sponge Puppet when it is time to clean up the classroom. Use the puppet to encourage children to put away toys and organize materials. Have the puppet lead children in singing the following version of "Here We Go 'Round the Mulberry Bush" as they work:

This is the way we clean up our room,
Clean up our room,
Clean up our room.
This is the way we clean up our room
*On a busy **Wednesday morning**.*

Change the boldfaced words to reflect the day of the week and time of the day.

Cleanup

Dilly, the Duster Puppet

Materials
glue gun
wiggly eyes
pom-pom ball
duster
ribbon

Directions
Glue a pair of wiggly eyes and a pom-pom ball for a nose to a duster. Tie a ribbon into a bow, and glue it to the lower part of the duster where a neck would be.

Variation
Rearrange the facial features and omit the bow to create a porcupine puppet.

Reading Recommendations
Little Rabbit Foo-Foo by Michael Rosen
Mr. Tickle by Roger Hargreaves
Number One, Tickle Your Tum by John Prater
The Tickle Octopus by Audrey Wood
Tickle, Tickle by Helen Oxenbury

Song Suggestions
"Little Rabbit Foo-Foo" from *Great Big Hits* by Sharon, Lois, and Bram (Drive)
"Ten Fingers" from *Making Moosic* by Anna Moo (Anna Moo Good Moo's Productions)

Tickle a Friend

Materials

none

Arrange children in a circle, and hand Dilly to a child. Chant the following verse, and encourage the child holding the puppet to gently follow the directions for tickling the person beside him or her:

*Tickle a friend's **toes**,*
*Tickle the **toes** next to you.*
Tickle a friend's toes,
And laugh—ha ha!

After the verse, direct the child to hand the puppet to the person who was just tickled. Change the boldfaced word to a new body part, and have the class repeat the activity until each child has handled the puppet.

Little Tickle Foo-Foo

Materials

none

Use Dilly to direct children to wash their hands. Use the puppet to gently "tickle" children as you sing the following verse to the tune of "Little Bunny Foo-Foo":

Little Tickle Foo-Foo
Hopping through the classroom
*Tickled **Nita's nose***
*And said, **"Go wash your hands."***

Repeat the verse until each child has been tickled and directed to wash his or her hands. Change the boldfaced words of the verse to reflect another child, body part, and direction (e.g., *Tickled Sammy's belly/And said, "Go find your mat"*).

Cleanup

Bumblebee Paper-Plate Puppet

Materials
scissors
yellow and black felt
paper plate
glue gun
paint-stirring stick
buttons
pipe cleaner
clear plastic sheet protector

Directions
Cut yellow felt so that it will cover a paper plate, and glue it in place. Glue strips of black felt in a curve across the plate. Cut more black felt so that it will cover a paint-stirring stick, and glue it in place. Fold the plate in half (felt side out), insert the paint-stirring stick, and glue the edges of the plate together. Cut out two circles from black felt for a head, and glue them to one end of the stick. Glue on button eyes and pipe-cleaner antennae. Cut a clear plastic sheet protector into the shape of wings, and glue them on the back of the puppet.

Variation
Use light-blue or black felt to create a dragonfly or mosquito puppet.

Reading Recommendations
The Bee Tree by Patricia Polacco
The Honey Bee and the Robber by Eric Carle
Honey Bee's Busy Day by R. Fowler

Song Suggestions
"Baby Bumblebee" from *Sing Along Stew* by Linda Arnold (Youngheart Music)
"I Hear a Bee" from *Making Moosic* by Anna Moo (Anna Moo Good Moo's Productions)

Busy Bees

Materials
> none

Use the Bumblebee Paper-Plate Puppet to tell children *It's time for all the bumblebees to get busy cleaning up.* Or, help children focus on their work by having the puppet say *Look at my busy bees making patterns with their beads* or *A busy bee works until he or she is finished.*

How to "Bee" a Good Helper

Materials
> Bee pattern (page 144)
> scissors
> crayons or markers
> white butcher paper
> yellow construction paper
> stapler
> honey graham crackers

Make several copies of the Bee pattern, and cut out the bees. Invite children to color the bee cutouts. Cover a bulletin board with white butcher paper. Add a yellow construction paper beehive and the title *We Can "Bee" Good Helpers.* Ask children to name ways that they can be good helpers. Staple a bee cutout onto the board every time someone in class demonstrates how to be a good helper. When the class earns a set number of bee cutouts, reward children with a sweet treat of honey graham crackers.

Mouth

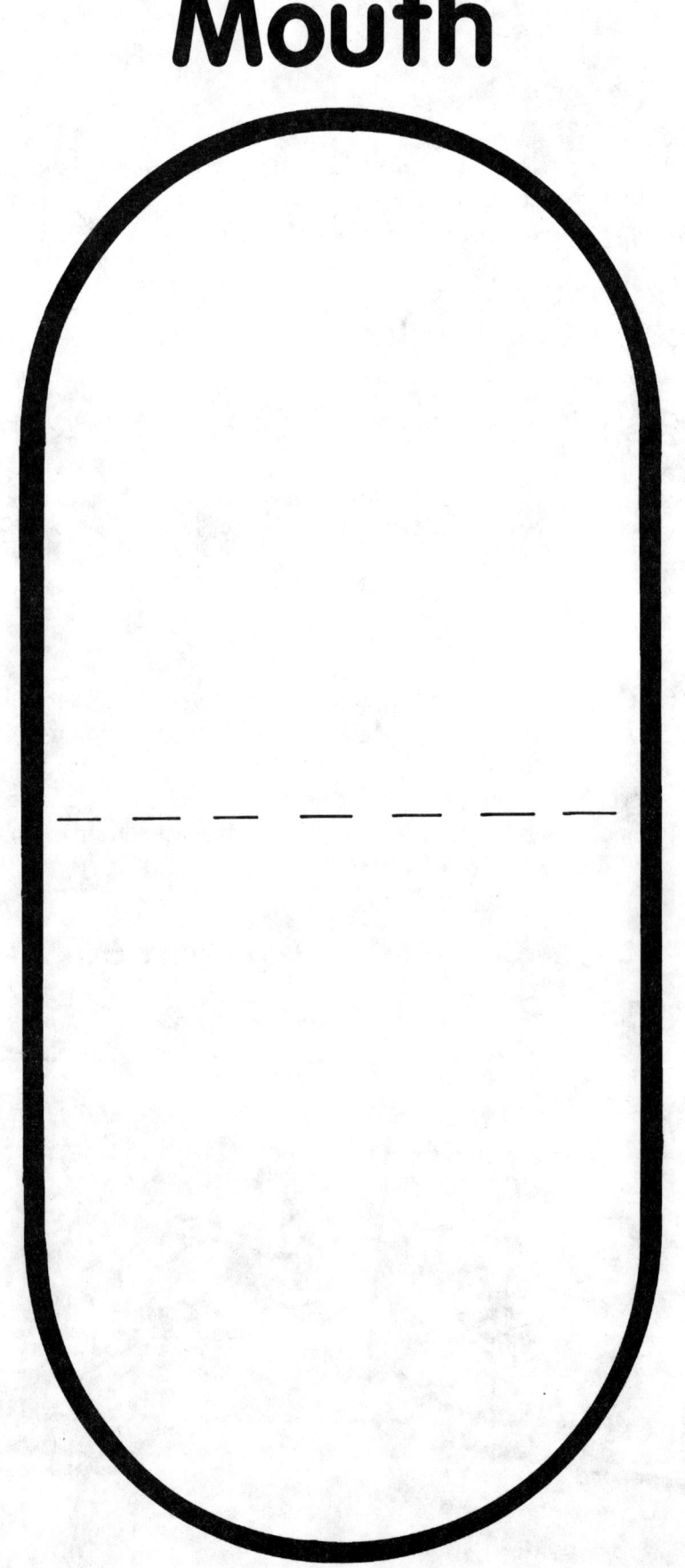

Bear

Body

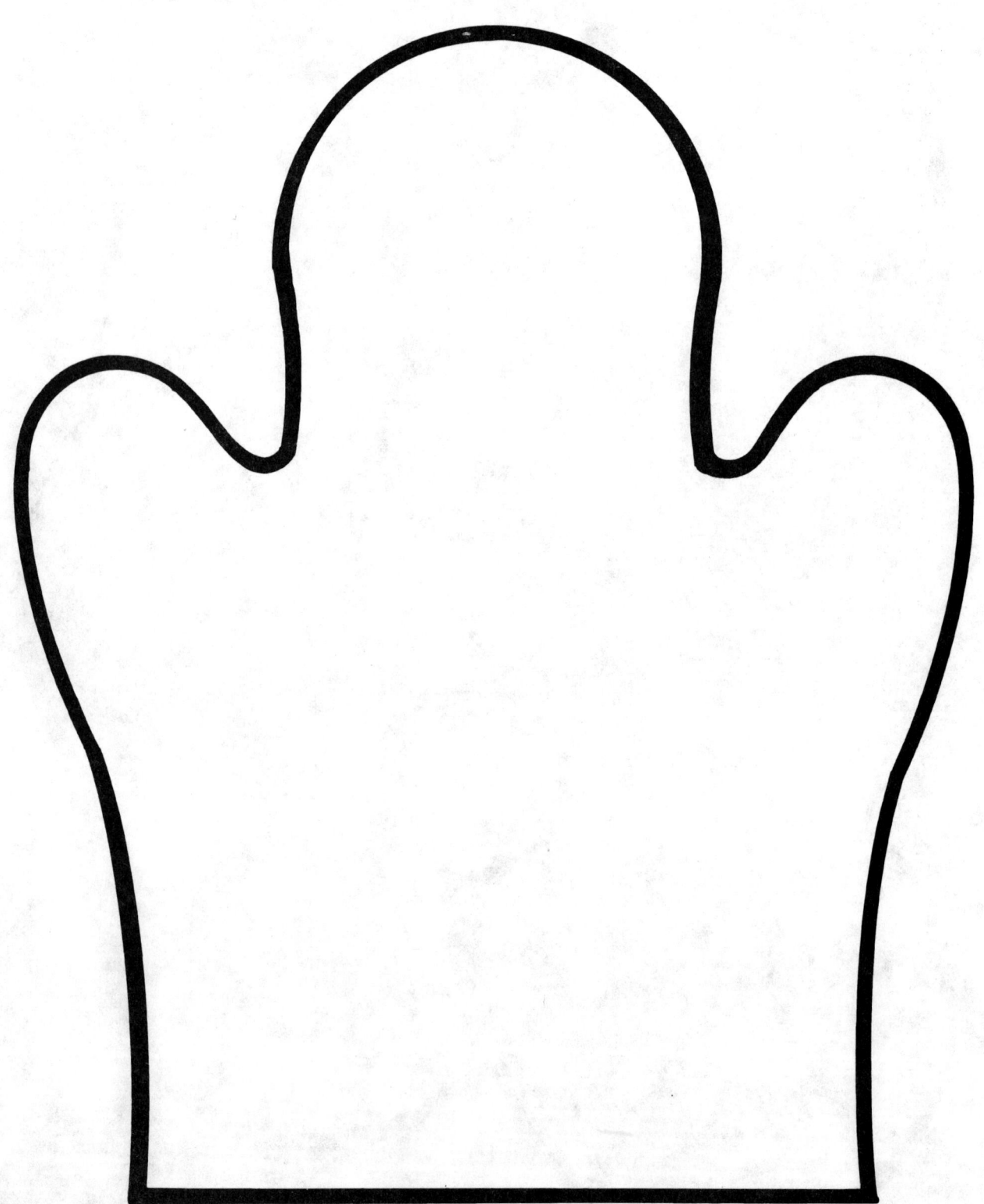

Sergeant Shape

Clown

Bottle Body

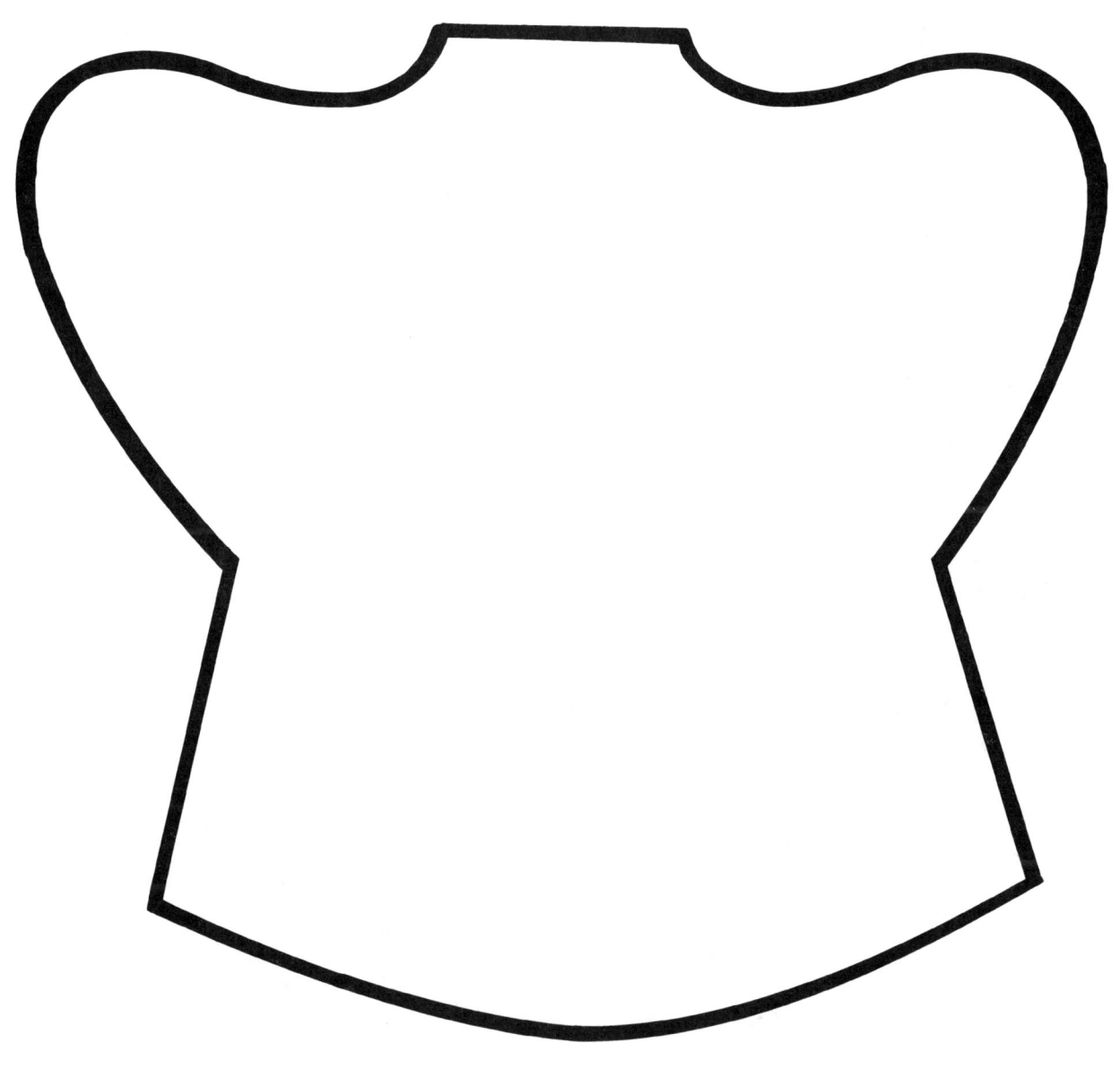

Fish

Turkey and Feather

Garden

Elephant

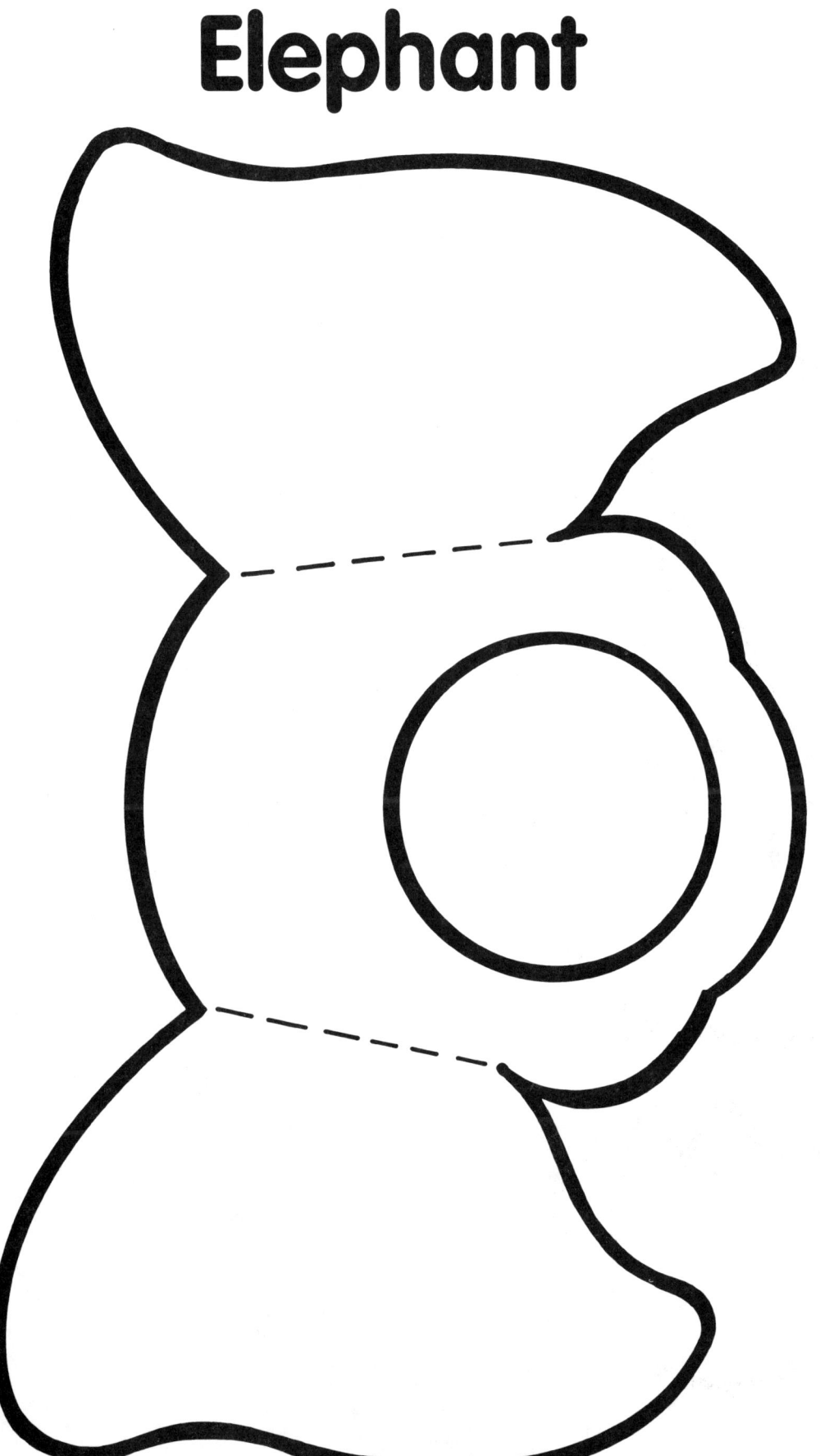

Spikes

Camel

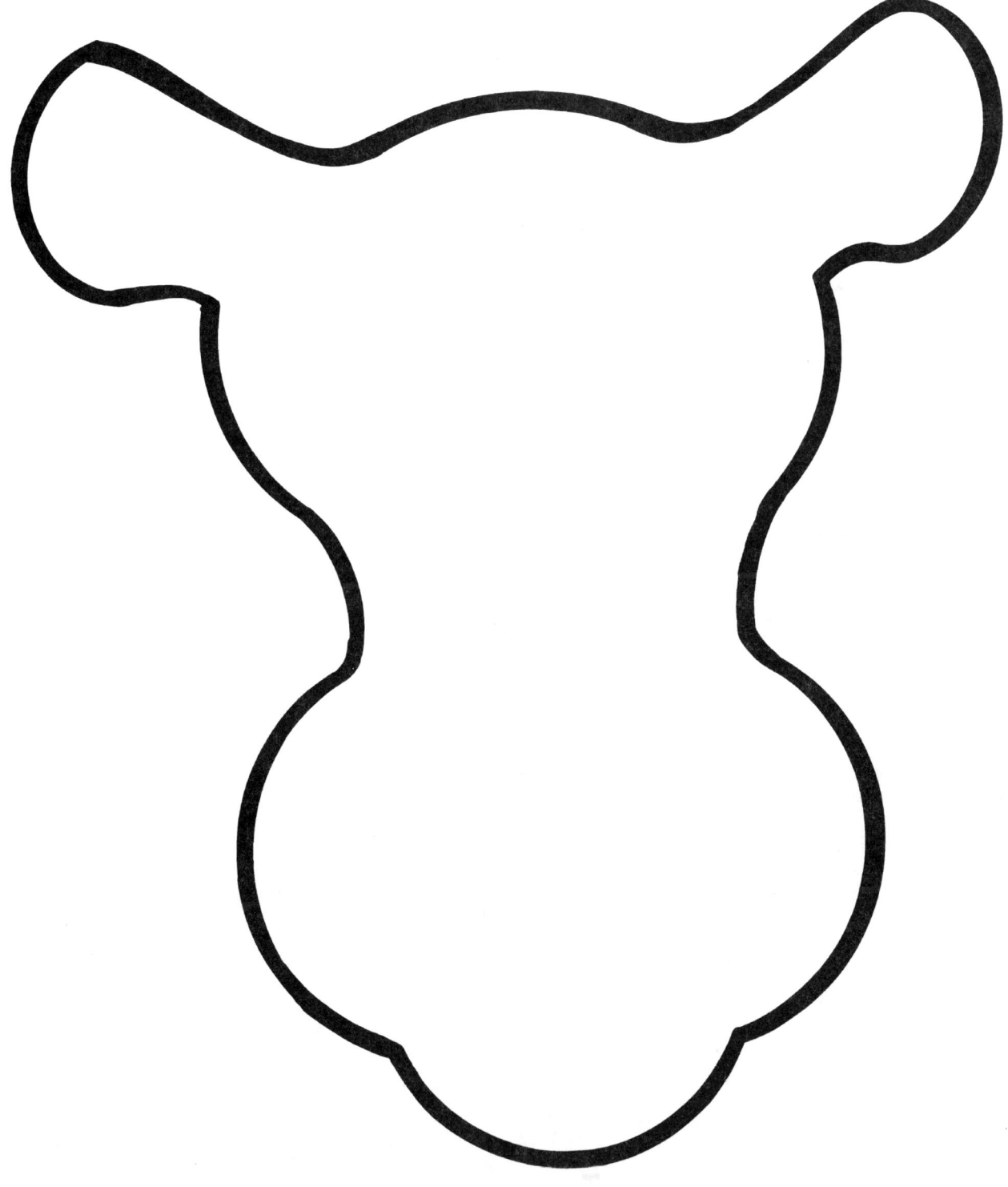

Lion

Gorilla

Penguin

Cat

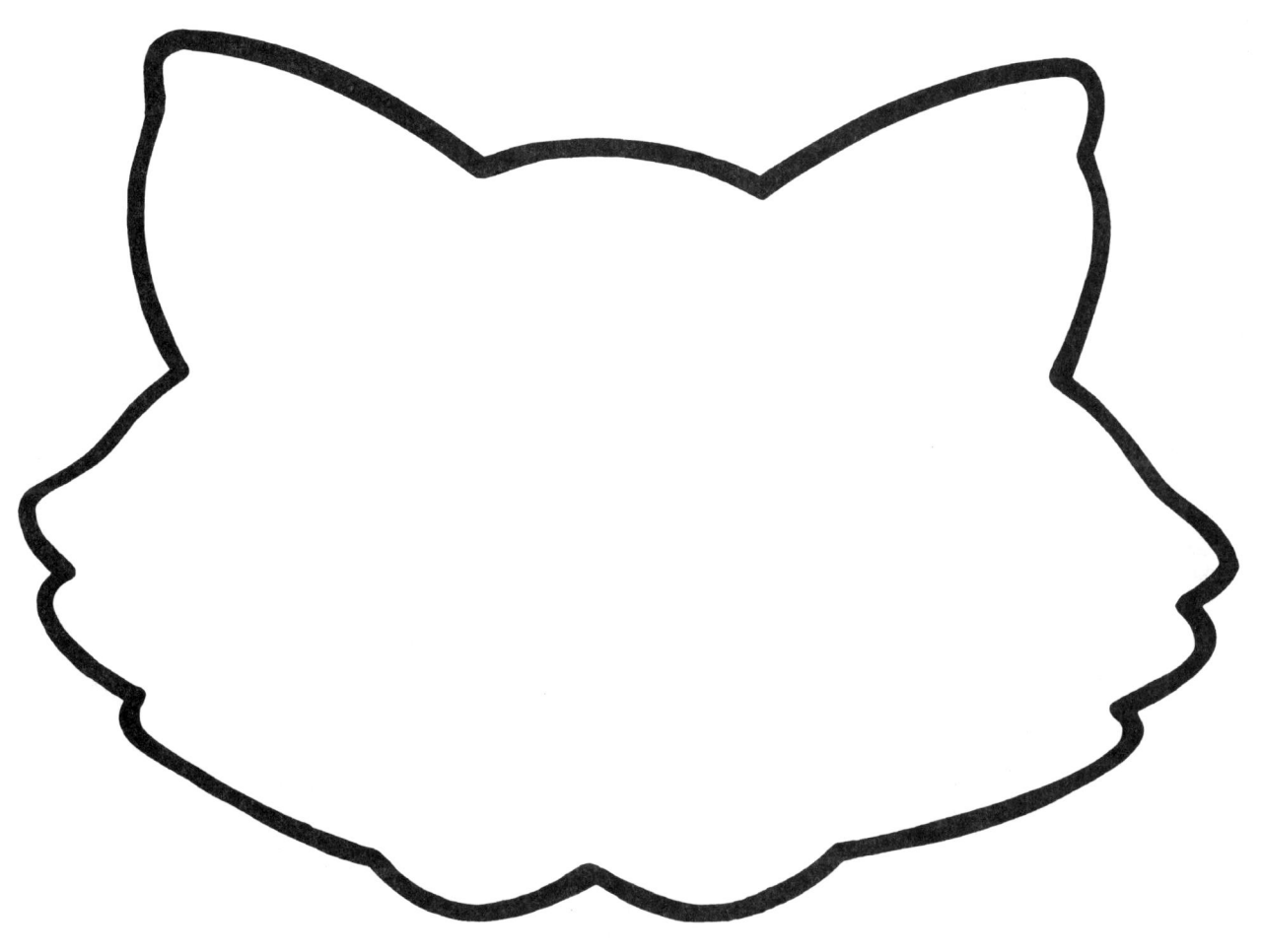

Butterfly

Nose

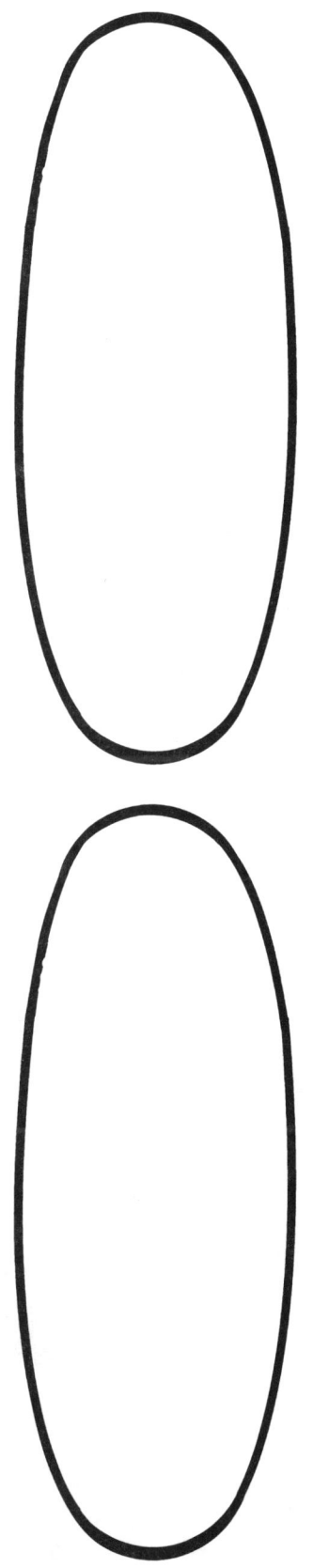

Bee